November 20

# The
# Isle of
# Purbeck

## Guide Book

### by Charles Tait

ISBN 9781909036338

# The Isle of Purbeck Guide Book
## First Edition
©copyright Charles Tait 2015
Published by Charles Tait
Kelton, St Ola, Orkney KW15 1TR
Tel 01856 873738  Fax 01856 875313
charles.tait@zetnet.co.uk
charles-tait.co.uk

Printing by Martins the Printers, Berwick-upon-Tweed

*Gad Cliff and Kimmeridge Bay from Tyneham Cap*

# The Isle of Purbeck

## Guide Book

### by Charles Tait

*This book is dedicated to my cousins Kirsten Leonard and Jean Buckland*

**ACKNOWLEDGEMENTS**

During the years of work on the research, photography, design and production of *The Dorset Guide Book* many people, books, websites, publications and bodies have been consulted. The author would like to thank everyone for their assistance.

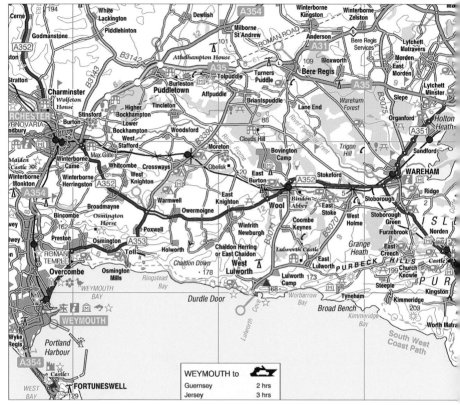

THE ISLE OF PURBECK (OE *pūr bic* Bittern beak, referring to the shape) is in fact a peninsula. This book uses the local government district boundaries. This covers c.156m² (404km²) and had a population of 45,200 in 2011.

The coastline runs from the White Nothe in the west to Lytchett Bay near Poole in the east. It then loops northwest to take in Charborough Park, before passing north of the A35 and heading back to the coast, east of Tolpuddle.

In former times the Isle of Purbeck was much smaller. A 1370 Corfe Castle document stated that, *"The whole Isle of Purbeck is a warren of our Lord the King and pertains to his said castle. It extends from Flouresberi (Flowers Barrow) to*

*Administrative districts of Dorset*

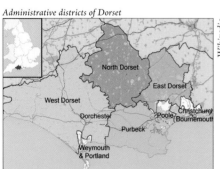

*Studland Church*

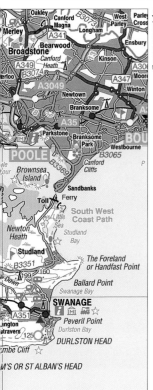

*until it again reaches the aforesaid place of Flouresberi"*

**Geology** The Purbeck Hills are part of a Cretaceous chalk ridge that runs from the White Nothe to the Old Harry Rocks. There are many spectacular features along the coast including the resplendent chalk cliffs. These run from the White Nothe to Worbarrow Bay and reappear at Ballard Down.

Further east the cliffs are mostly of Jurassic rocks, including Portland limestone, Purbeck marble and the Kimmeridge beds. Extensive quarrying was done on the cliffs near Swanage and inland. Vast amounts were used in London and elsewhere. The Jurassic Coast World Heritage Site includes the coast from the White Nothe to Old Harry Rocks.

To the north of the Purbeck Hills there are huge deposits of Eocene Purbeck ball clay. This has been extracted since at least the Iron Age for the making of pottery. During Roman times this became a major industry. Clay from here is still used in the Staffordshire potteries.

*the wood of Wytewey and thence as far as Luggerford, from that to the bridge of Wareham, and so along the sea, in an easterly direction, to a place called the Castle of Stodland; thence by the sea-coast to the chapel of St Aldhalm, and from thence west*

*Old Harry Rocks at the east end of Ballard Down from seaward*

# Welcome to The Isle of Purbeck

*Durdle Door is one of Dorset's most iconic features*

**Natural History** With Chalk and Limestone downlands, extensive areas of lowland heath and its long coast, Purbeck offers a great deal for those who are interested in wildlife. Of the many nature reserves, Durlston Country Park, Ballard Down, Studland, Arne, and Higher Hyde Heath are essential visits.

Many come to see the rare Early-Spider Orchids in bloom at Durlston, or Dartford Warblers and scarce reptiles at Arne. Places such are Higher Hyde Heath are excellent for butterflies and dragonflies. The Lulworth Skipper butterfly can be found on the southeastern coast where its larval host, Tor-grass, grows.

**Natural Features** along the coast include Lulworth Cove, Durdle Door, Kimmeridge and the Old Harry Rocks. In fact the whole coastline from the White Nothe to Studland Bay offers dramatic vistas. All can be taken in by means of the South West Coast Path and the many trails which join it.

*Dartford Warbler*

*Lulworth Skipper*

Wikipedia

*Early-spider Orchid*

Wikimedia

**Beaches** Both Swanage and Studland Bays have extensive, safe sandy beaches. Swanage is an attractive seaside resort, less developed and busy than Weymouth or Bournemouth. It retains a fine ambience in a quiet way. Studland is much less developed, but also much busier, due to its proximity to Poole. With especially lovely sands, backed by dunes, woods and heathland, this beach is one of the very best in Dorset.

**Archaeology** The oldest evidence for the presence of people is Palaeolithic handaxes from 400,000 years ago. Dorset has been continuously inhabited since c.11,000BC when the first Mesolithic hunter-gatherers arrived after the last glaciation.

Neolithic, Bronze and Iron Age cultures flourished. Romans, Saxons, Vikings, Normans and others came and went. Great monasteries were founded and dissolved, fine small towns were built and agriculture thrived. Later, the British military arrived in the 19th century. Dorset has withstood and absorbed them all.

**Visitor Attractions** Purbeck offers a wide range of man-made places to visit. These include the romantic ruins of Corfe Castle, the walled Saxon town of Wareham and Tyneham, "The Village That Time Forgot". The Saxon and Norman churches at Wareham and Studland are especially good examples of their type.

**Museums** The Tank Museum is stunningly excellent and quite unmissable. Aficionados will find the Swanage Steam Railway a great way to spend time experiencing old fashioned locomotives and rolling stock. Of the many small and quirky museums, perhaps the tiny Clouds Hill is the most poignant. TE Lawrence (of Arabia) used it as his base from 1923 to 1935.

**Walking** Purbeck is ideal walking country and offers a huge variety of options. These range from signposted trails to short town tours and much longer routes. There are many options for circular walks, from the easy to the challenging. The dorsetforyou.com website has many walks suggestions for Purbeck, including downloadable maps and itineraries at - dorsetforyou.com/walking/purbeck

The Discover Purbeck Information Centre in Wareham Library has walks leaflets and a great deal more information about what to do and see in Purbeck. Walks can be downloaded from this website as pdf files and printed out.

### The Origin of the Name "Dorset"

Although Dorset is mentioned in the *Anglo-Saxon Chronicle* in AD891, the root name is very much older. Many variations occur, but all include the prefix dorn, (B *durno-*, large round pebble or fist). The Romans called Dorchester *Durnovaria*, most likely from the original local name. Maiden Castle, the large Iron Age fort 1.6mi (2.5km) southwest of Dorchester may be the *Dunium* (B *dun*, fort) referred to by Ptolemy c.AD150 as the main stronghold of the *Durotriges*.

Interestingly, over 40,000 sling shot pebbles were found at Maiden Castle when excavated. Whether this has anything to do with the name is unknown, but it adds to the mystery.

The Roman name was probably pronounced as *Dornawara* by the locals. Later, the Saxons added a suffix (OE *ceaster*, town) to give *Dornwaraceaster*, soon shortened to Dorchester. This led to the local people being referred to as the *Dornsæte* (OE *sæte*, people), and hence to the modern Dorset.

*Chapman's Pool*

*View eastwards from the White Nothe*

*Lulworth Cove*

*Durdle Door*

*Worbarrow Bay*

**The Dorset Coastline** offers spectacular options for visitors. The dramatic Jurassic Coast stretches from Exmouth in Devon to Old Harry Rocks. Further east uninterrupted beautiful sands stretch for a further 12mi (19km).

**Sea Temperatures** at Weymouth peak around 18.5°C in early September, which is very pleasant for swimming. For most of July , August and September they exceed 16°C. In January and February the average sea temperature is 4°C.

**The White Nothe** overlooks Weymouth Bay and marks the start of Purbeck. From here to the Old Harry Rocks is 30mi (48km). This part of the Jurassic Coast consists of dramatic chalk and limestone cliffs with lovely bays, sea stacks, natural arches and other features.

**Durdle Door** is perhaps the most iconic symbol of this coast, along with its neighbour, Lulworth Cove. Both exceed expectations despite their popularity. The coast paths and shingle beaches here should not be missed.

**Worbarrow Bay** can only be accessed when the Lulworth Ranges are open. Apart from the ruined village of Tyneham, there are wonderful walks along the cliffs to Lulworth Cove and to Kimmeridge Bay with its famous rock strata.

**Durlston Head** is the southeast extremity of Purbeck. The nature reserve here is one of the best in the whole country for rare butterflies and plants. It is also a hotspot for migrating birds. The highlights include Lulworth Skippers and Chalk-hill Blue butterflies as well as Early-spider Orchids.

**Swanage** has a fine sandy beach, sheltered by the Purbeck Hills to the north and the coastal ridge to the south. It is the least commercial of all Dorset's resorts, but has a charm all of its own. With its steam railway, Pleasure Pier and surrounding countryside it has much to offer the visitor.

**Old Harry Rocks** are a series of chalk sea stacks at the east end of Ballard Down. They mark the eastern end of the Jurassic Coast World Heritage Site.

**Studland Bay**, one of the finest beaches in Dorset, extends over 4mi (6km) to South Haven Point. This beautiful arc of sand, backed by dunes, trees and a large heathland nature reserve, is uncommercialised, but very popular due to its proximity to Poole.

*Durlston Head*

*Swanage Bay*

*Old Harry Rocks*

*Studland Bay*

| BEST TEN BEACHES AND CLIFFS | |
|---|---|
| Chapman's Pool | 34 |
| Durlston Country Park | 38 |
| Kimmeridge Bay | 32 |
| Lulworth Cove & Durdle Door | 26 |
| Old Harry Rocks | 42 |
| Studland Bay | 43 |
| Swanage Bay | 40 |
| Tyneham Cap | 31 |
| White Nothe | 26 |
| Worbarrow Bay | 29 |

*The Tank Museum has machines dating from WWI onwards*

*Corfe Castle is one of the most romantic and spectacular in England*

*Swanage Steam Railway*

*Swanage Bay*

**VISITOR ATTRACTIONS** Dorset has a huge number of visitor attractions, from internationally important museums to tiny village heritage centres. A small selection of the "must visit" places are described here. Many more are included in the Gazetteer and the Information Pages at the back of the book.

**The Tank Museum** is, without a doubt, one of the best museums in the UK. With over 300 tanks and other military vehicles it will please any enthusiast, but the sheer quality of the displays will also impress the most unmilitary of folk. Not to be missed. Military vehicles from 1914 to the 21$^{st}$ century are on display, with live events during the year.

**Corfe Castle** in east Purbeck is probably the most romantic, spectacular and most visitable castle in the UK. It was established by the Normans, expanded over centuries and slighted by Oliver Cromwell. He only managed to create an even more special place to visit, despite his destruction. The village has many attractive old houses and buildings.

**Swanage Steam Railway** was set up after the British Rail branch line was closed in 1972. It operates a steam timetable from Corfe Castle to Swanage and hopes to have regular services to Wareham by 2015. Any steam enthusiast will be delighted by the old stations, locomotives and services, as are most children.

**Tyneham** was requisitioned in 1943 during the lead-up to D-Day and remains part of the MoD Lulworth Ranges. Situated in an isolated and sheltered valley, this abandoned village can only be visited when the Ranges are open to the public. There are marked paths down to Warbarrow Bay, east to Kimmeridge Bay and west to Lulworth Cove.

*Lulworth Cove from the east*

**TE Lawrence** first came to Dorset in 1923 when he joined the Tank Corp at Bovington Camp. He rented and later bought Clouds Hill, now owned by the National Trust The Lawrence of Arabia Trail is a 7mi (11km) circular walk starting at the Tank Museum, taking in the River Frome, Moreton and Clouds Hill.

*Tyneham Village*

**Monkey World Centre,** 1mi (1.5km) north of Wool, was founded in 1987 by Jim Cronin to house Chimpanzees rescued from Spanish beaches. Today this large (65ha) park has a wide range of Chimpanzees, Woolly Monkeys, Orangutans, Gibbons, Lemurs, Capuchins, Macaques and other monkeys to see.

*Clouds Hill*

*Monkey World*

| Best Ten Visitor Attractions | |
|---|---|
| Clouds Hill | 64 |
| Corfe Castle | 44 |
| Durdle Door | 26 |
| Monkey World | 66 |
| Sculpture by the Lake | 67 |
| Swanage | 40 |
| Swanage Railway | 41, 47 |
| Tank Museum | 62 |
| Tyneham | 31 |
| Wareham | 52 |

*Flowers Barrow above Worbarrow Bay*

**Ancient Dorset** There are a vast number of archaeological and prehistorical sites in Dorset. Many were dug into in the 19th century by gentlemen antiquarians and some have been more scientifically excavated in modern times.

Very few such places are signposted or presented to the public to visit. To many this simply increases the challenge and satisfaction of finding and experiencing ancient sites. Throughout the book Ordnance Survey coordinates are quoted to aid visitors.

**Palaeolithic Age** The first evidence of people in Dorset is handaxes dating from at least 400,000 years ago found in gravel deposits beside rivers. There are no sites to visit, but several museums have displays including those in Dorchester, Poole and Christchurch.

**Mesolithic Age** At the start of the last inter-glacial period around 11,000BC people started to arrive over the land bridge to Europe as the climate warmed up. They left many traces of shelters, hearths and piles of shells.

**Neolithic Age** Dorset has many remains from the time of the first farmers from c.4000BC onwards. These include causewayed camps, burial mounds, enclosures, ditches and banks. They also built henges, some of which were huge. Sadly only vestiges of these remain. Pottery as well as stone and bone tools can be seen in the museums.

**Bronze Age** There are funerary barrows, dating from c.2000BC and later, all over the county. Some yielded exceptionally rich grave goods when dug into in the 19th century. There are remains of farms, field systems and settlements in many areas.

**Iron Age** Starting c.6000BC hillforts were constructed in large numbers all over Dorset, some on the site of previous Neolithic enclosures such as at Maiden Castle. They vary in size and complexity but all are hilltops defended by massive ramparts and ditches and enclose roundhouse settlements.

**The Romans** rapidly took over the whole of southern England after their invasion of AD43, including Dorset. Their roads are still very prominent in the landscape, especially Ackling Dyke. Villas, mosaics, temples, forts, harbours, weapons, tools, pottery and household artefacts have all been found.

*Mesolithic arrowheads and flints in Wareham Museum*

*Carved jet ware in Wareham Museum*

**The Saxons** took control of Dorset by the late 7th century. By the end of the 9th century Wessex was fully established under Alfred the Great. Abbeys such as Shaftesbury were founded and many churches were built.

The ancient churches at Wareham and Studland have many Saxon features. The impressive wall built by Alfred to defend the town from the Danes still surrounds Wareham and makes a fine circular walk.

*Wareham Saxon Town Wall*

**The Normans**, who were really Vikings masquerading as Frenchmen took over a highly organised country in 1066. Dorset has many churches and abbeys built by them, usually on the site of earlier Saxon chapels.

*Studland Saxon and Norman church*

There are only a very few ruined castles from this time, most having long since fallen out of use and been demolished. Corfe Castle is Dorset's best example. Founded by William I, it met its nemesis in Oliver Cromwell.

*Corfe Castle*

*Bere Regis church roof*

| Best Ten Historical Sites | |
|---|---|
| Clouds Hill | 64 |
| Corfe Castle | 44 |
| Durdle Door | 26 |
| Monkey World | 66 |
| Sculpture by the Lake | 67 |
| Swanage | 40 |
| Swanage Railway | 41, 47 |
| Tank Museum | 62 |
| Tyneham | 31 |
| Wareham | 52 |

Avocets at Brownsea Island

*Anvil Point, Durlston Country Park*

*Arne RSPB Reserve*

*Upper Hyde Heath*

*Tadnoll Heath*

**Purbeck**, with its chalk and limestone rocks, heathland, clifftops, sheltered shorelines and clay areas, has many superb places to find wildlife. There is a host of nature reserves and other wild places, some remote, others right in the middle of towns.

**Durlston Country Park**, near Swanage, with its wild flower meadows, orchids and butterflies is one of the best wildlife sites in Dorset. Many come to seek the Early-spider and other Orchids as well as rare butterflies such as the Lulworth Skipper and Chalk-hill Blue. The Castle is a Visitor Centre with interactive displays, a shop and restaurant.

**Arne RSPB Reserve**, east of Wareham, is prime Dorset heathland and vies strongly with Durlston as an essential visit. This is a top class nature reserve worth visiting at all times of year. It is prime habitat for Dartford Warblers, Nightjars and Woodlarks. All six species of British reptiles are present as well as many dragonflies.

**Lulworth Cove** and nearby Durdle Door are Dorset icons. They are formed of hard Portland Limestone, which as been folded and eroded into fantastical shapes. The West Lulworth Heritage Centre tells the story of the formation of this coast. Rare plants including Rock Sea-lavender and butterflies such as Lulworth Skipper are found here.

**Ballard Down** forms the eastern end of the Purbeck Hills chalk ridge. A 5mi (8km) circular walk starting at Studland offers spectacular views over the Old Harry Rocks, Swanage Bay and north to Studland Bay. The southern slopes are a prime site for rare butterflies such as the Adonis Blue and Lulworth Skipper, as well as many wild flowers.

**Studland NNR** has heathland, sand dunes, peat bog, carr and shallow freshwater lagoons. Rare species here include the Dartford Warbler, Nightjar ands all six species of native reptiles. It also holds many dragonflies and bees. In winter, large flocks of wildfowl and waders mass here.

**Brownsea Island** is the largest island in Poole Harbour. Belonging to the National Trust, it can be reached by ferry from Poole or Wareham. The varied habitats include woodland, marshy areas, saltmarsh and a large lagoon. Red Squirrels survive here and many Avocets overwinter. Grey Herons, Little Egrets, Common and Sandwich Terns all nest here.

*Tilly Whim Caves, Durston Country Park*

*Swanage from Ballard Down*

*Studland Heath and Poole Harbour from Kingswood Down*

*Brownsea Island*

| Best Ten Nature Sites | |
|---|---:|
| Arne RSPB Reserve | 54 |
| Ballard Down | 42 |
| Brownsea Island | 56 |
| Durlston Country Park | 38 |
| Higher Hyde Reserve | 67 |
| Kimmeridge Bay | 32 |
| Lulworth | 26 |
| Poole Harbour | 43, 54 |
| St Alhelm's Chapel | 34 |
| Studland Heath | 43 |

# Jurassic Coast UNESCO World Heritage Site

**The "Jurassic Coast"** Dorset and East Devon World Heritage Site extends for about 95mi (155km) from Orcombe Point near Exmouth in Devon to Old Harry Rocks near Swanage in Purbeck, Dorset. It was inscribed by UNESCO in 2001 on account of its exposures of the geology of the Mesozoic Period.

The World Heritage Site is a narrow strip of coastline stretching from the lowest spring ebb to the tops of the adjacent cliffs. Known as the "Jurassic Coast", it includes exposures from the whole of the Mesozoic Period, including the Triassic (252-201Ma, Jurassic (201-145Ma) and Cretaceous (145-66Ma) Periods.

During the Triassic Period the area was part of *Pangea*, which formed most of the land mass at the time. It was a hot desert through which rivers flowed from high mountains further west. Large lakes formed periodically and huge areas of alluvial deposits formed.

Though fossils from the Triassic are uncommon, it was a period of great diversification and evolution. Dinosaurs and many other four-legged animals, including early mammals, developed. Plants similarly had a great renewal after the mass extinctions of the Permian Period.

*Ammonite*

*Ichthyosaur*

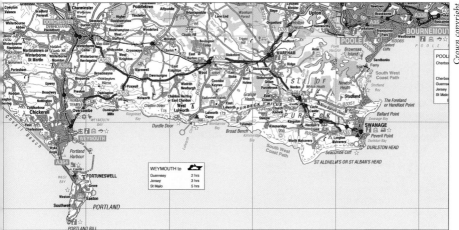

The Jurassic Period saw great changes as *Pangea* split into today's continents. The climate and sea level fluctuated in synchrony with solar cycles, resulting in a variety of sediments ranging from clays and sandstones to limestones. Fossils from this period are numerous and include ammonites, belemnites and many reptiles.

During the early Cretaceous Period the area was covered by swamps and lagoons. Later, earth movements lowered and tilted the region from west to east. Once more it was covered by the sea. Chalk was formed from the skeletal remains of algae.

When the land was once more uplifted above sea level, erosion resumed, exposing the oldest Mesozoic sediments in the west and creating river valleys. Later still, the area was once more submerged and covered by clays and sands which sit "unconformably" on top of the earlier layers of sediments. This is well seen near the tops

of the cliffs at Branscombe and Golden Cap.

During the Cretaceous Period the land was dominated by dinosaurs and other reptiles. The seas teemed with molluscs such as ammonites and belemnites as well as aquatic dinosaurs, including examples of Ichthyosaurs and Plesiosaurs.

*Dinosaur Footprint*

*Kimmeridge Shale*

*Worbarrow Bay, Isle of Purbeck*

19     *Purbeck Guide Book 1st edition by Charles Tait*

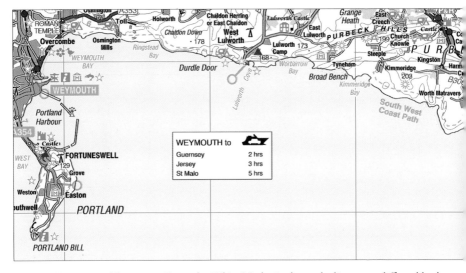

| WEYMOUTH to | |
|---|---|
| Guernsey | 2 hrs |
| Jersey | 3 hrs |
| St Malo | 5 hrs |

**Isle of Purbeck** The east coast of Portland is lower and less rugged than the west, with landslides, old quarries and several coves. Portland Harbour and Weymouth Bay are both sheltered by the "Isle".

**White Cliffs** From Ringstead Bay eastward the cliffs are composed of chalk, limestones, sandstones and clays from the Upper Jurassic Period. Shale is exposed, most notably at Kimmeridge Bay, while oil has been found in eastern Purbeck and seeps from the rocks near Ringstead Bay.

From the White Nothe in the west to Ballard Down and the Old Harry Rocks in the east, the Purbeck coastline is spectacular. Burning Cliff, above Ringstead Bay, is named from a landslip of 1826, when shale was ignited by exposed iron pyrites and subsequently burned for months.

**Durdle Door** is a natural arch formed from limestone which has been tilted almost vertical. Nearby there are several spectacular areas of contorted rocks, most notably at Lulworth Cove. Here the sea has found a weak point in

the limestone cliffs and broken through to form a circular bay, backed by chalk cliffs.

**Kimmeridge Bay** has thick exposures of fossil-rich clay and shales formed beneath a tropical ocean, 155Ma ago. There are frequent rock falls. Spontaneous combustion of the shale can occur when it is freshly exposed to the air. The bay is a marine nature reserve.

**Purbeck Limestone** was quarried from ancient times in many places, including at Seacombe, Winspit and Dancing Ledge. Many fossils of

*View east from the White Nothe*

*Stair Hole near Lulworth Cove*

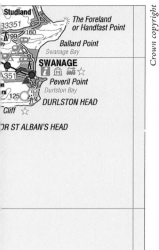

*Crown copyright*

*Old Harry Rocks from the east*

*Kimmeridge Bay from the west*

fish, reptiles and V early small mammals occur in the Purbeck Beds. Dinosaur footprints have also been found, some about a metre across.

Further east, St Adhelm's Head reaches over 100m in height. From here spectacular cliffs run west to Chapman's Pool and east towards Durlston Head, where a fault drops the limestone to nearly sea level.

**Old Harry Rocks** On the north side of Swanage Bay, the chalk ridge which forms the backbone of the Isle of Purbeck ends in Ballard Down.

*The Durdle Door*

The Jurassic Coast ends at The Foreland or Handfast Point, with its off-lying and picturesque Old Harry Rocks.

*Worbarrow Bay*

| Jurassic Coast Ringstead Bay to Old Harry Rocks | |
|---|---|
| Ringstead Bay | 26 |
| White Nothe | 26 |
| Durdle Door | 26 |
| Lulworth Cove | 26 |
| Worbarrow Bay | 29 |
| Kimmeridge | 32 |
| St Aldhelm's Head | 34 |
| Durlston Head | 38 |
| Swanage | 40 |
| Old Harry Rocks | 42 |

*Sunset over Bat's Head from Durdle Door*

# The Isle of Purbeck

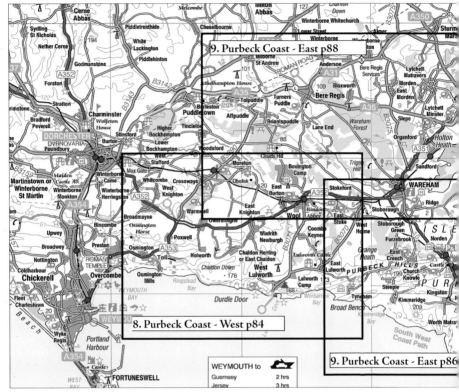

9. Purbeck Coast - East p88

8. Purbeck Coast - West p84

9. Purbeck Coast - East p86

WEYMOUTH to
Guernsey     2 hrs
Jersey       3 hrs

**The Isle of Purbeck** has such a lot to offer the visitor that would take a lifetime to appreciate all of its charms. It is a paradise for walkers, cyclists and nature lovers. Its world-class nature reserves are essential for those interested in birds, reptiles, butterflies, dragonflies and wild flowers.

**The Gazetteer** follows the coastline anticlockwise from the White Nothe to Wareham and then inland westwards. All of the main sites of interest are listed in the mini index opposite. The main Index, Suggested Itineraries and Places to Visit all include page references for ease of navigation.

**Suggested Itineraries** take in all of the main places of interest in West Coast Purbeck, East Coast Purbeck and Inland Purbeck. These are designed to help visitors plan their visits in advance, with extra information on distances, access, when to visit, etc.

*Corfe Castle c.1900*

*Wareham c.1910*

Crown copyright

*Silver-studded Blue*

*Black-tailed Godwit*

*Golden Samphire*

*Durdle Door*

*Old Harry Rocks and Handfast Point*

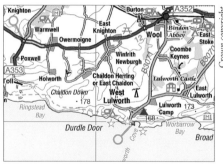

*Looking east from the White Nothe*

**The Coastline** between the White Nothe and Lulworth Cove comprises of spectacular undulating chalk and limestone cliffs. The 9mi (14km) circular walk starting at Ringstead Bay, Durdle Door or Lulworth Cove makes a very satisfying day out.

**The White Nothe** (OE *hnop*, peak, nose SY773810, 169m) marks the southwesterly tip of Purbeck. There are fine views to the east along spectacular chalk cliffs over Swyre Head to Lulworth. Looking to the west offers an impressive panoramic view of Ringstead Bay, Weymouth and Portland.

**Swyre Head** (OE *swēora*, neck, 98m) is about 2.5mi (4km) east along the undulating coastal path. The steep-sided little valley of Scratchy Bottom allows access to the shingle beach.

**Durdle Door** (OE *thyrelod duru*, thirl or pierced door, SY805802) is one of the most photographed coastal features in the UK. Even so to see it on a beautiful summer's evening is much better than anything that an image can convey. This natural arch is formed from an outcrop of near vertical Portland Limestone strata. There is a shingle beach here which can be followed west to Bat's Head with its own natural arch. St Oswald's Bay has a similar accessible shore with offlying ledges.

**Lulworth Cove** (OE *Lulla worð*, Lulla's Enclosure, SY825800) is about 1.5mi (2km) further east. This circular bay was formed when the sea broke through the Portland Limestone and eroded away the softer clay behind it. The

*Swyre Head and Bat's Hole from the east*

*The Crumple*

*Stair Hole*

landward side is part of the chalk backbone of Purbeck.

**Stair Hole and the Crumple** are dramatic demonstrations of the effects of the sea and of much earlier violent earth movements. Eventually the central, pierced, barrier will collapse and the bay will be opened up like its neighbour. The amazing contortions in the Portland Limestone are best seen in low evening light.

**West Lulworth Heritage Centre** has excellent displays on the geology, archaeology and history of the Cove. The Jurassic Jaws section has an Ichthyosaur skeleton, huge Plesiosaur jaws and fish fossils. There is also a gift shop with local produce, maps and guides.

**Lulworth Castle** dates from the 17th century. It was bought by Humphrey Weld in 1641, and remains in the same family today. The castle suffered a severe fire in 1929, which wrecked the interior. It was partially restored eventually by government agencies and opened to visitors in 1998. It is surrounded by open grounds and woodland.

*Lulworth Cove in 1822 by William Daniell*

*Lulworth Cove with a steamer from an old postcard*

*Lulworth Cove from the west*

*Lulworth Castle in the mist*

*Lulworth Castle kitchen*

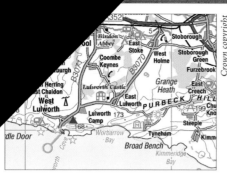

*Crown copyright*

*Worbarrow Bay from the east with Bindon Hill, Mupe B*

**Lulworth Ranges** All of the places described on the next four pages are within the MoD ranges, which are closed when in use. The coast path and range walks are open on most weekends and holidays, as well as all of August. Visitors must stick to the marked paths. Full information is available online or from Lulworth Range Control Office, Tel 01929 404819.

**The Fossil Forest** (SY832797) lies just east of Lulworth Cove but within the military area. Here, stromatolites, formed by cyanobacteria, grew in shallow seas and surrounded the trunks of trees killed by rising sea levels.

**Bindon Hill** (168m) was the site of the eponymous 12th century abbey, later moved to Wool in 1172. Today it is one of the best places to seek Lulworth Skipper butterflies. There are splendid views to the east from the several paths that cross Bindon Hill or follow the dramatic cliffs.

**Mupe Bay** (OE hōp, small bay) is backed by 140m chalk cliffs. Rocks and ledges on the southern side make for spectacular breaking seas during southwesterly gales.

**Arish Mell** (OE *ears mell*, Bottom Down) is about 1,000m further east. This lovely shingle beach has high cliffs on each side but is inaccessible as it is fenced off. When Winfrith Nuclear Reactor Site was operational, radioactive waste was discharged into the sea here. The pipes traversed MoD land, then inaccessible to the public. During the 1950s and 1960s, nuclear safety was not a prime consideration. Contamination of rocks, shores and groundwater is likely.

**Flowers Barrow** SY866806) is an Iron Age hillfort on the top of the cliffs below Rings Hill. Erosion of the cliffs means that the southern part is being lost to the sea; ramparts and ditches surround the other three sides. Hut circles can be clearly seen within the fort.

*Range signpost*

*Warning sign*

*Flowers Barrow is being eroded as the cliff recedes*

*...Mell in the distance. Worbarrow Tout is on the left and Flowers Barrow to the right*

**Worbarrow Bay** (OE *waru beorg*, Watch Hill) forms the east side of this spectacular natural amphitheatre. Flowers Barrow Ridge is the western end of the Purbeck Hills, a chalk ridge that runs over 12mi (20km) east to Ballard Down and the Old Harry Rocks.

**Worbarrow Tout** (55m) forms the southeast bastion of the bay and is an excellent viewpoint. The rocks here are older than the chalks. Portland Limestones (150my) underlie Purbeck Beds (147my). The Tout and cliffs to the east are much folded. Some of the beds are rich in fossils, mostly molluscs, while others contain dinosaur footprints.

Gold Down overlooks Tyneham and Worbarrow Bay. It offers panoramic views over Tyneham, as well as Worbarrow Bay all the way to Bindon Hill, Mupe Bay and Portland.

### LULWORTH RANGES

The Tank Corps was formed in 1916. By 1917 Lulworth was in use for live firing and in 1918 the Gunnery School was established here. During the 1930s the area was greatly extended and Lulworth Camp developed.

As tank guns became more powerful the original range was proving inadequate. In 1943 Heath and Tyneham were requisitioned to allow training of large numbers of crews. This continued until 1945. The ranges have remained in constant use by the Army since armoured vehicles remain a crucial part of today's land forces.

Lulworth Camp is the base of the British Army Armoured Fighting Vehicle Gunnery School. The Ranges are used for live firing and cover 2,830ha between Lulworth Cove and Kimmeridge Bay. They stretch 4.5mi (7km) inland over a vast area of heathland. A safety zone extends several miles out to sea.

About 70,000 shells are fired annually, some of which fail to explode. Although the range walks are cleared before opening dangerous objects may be encountered and should on no account be touched. Unexploded shells also occasionally get washed up on the beaches and obviously must be avoided.

*The ranges are closed to the public when in use by the military. The coast path and range walks are open on most weekends and holidays, as well as all of August. Visitors must stick to the marked paths. Full information is available online or from Lulworth Range Control Office, Tel 01929 404819.*

*Arish Mell from Gold Down*

*Worbarrow Beach*

*Pondfield from Worbarrow Tout*

# Tyneham to Kimmeridge

*Panoramic view over Tyneham from*

**Tyneham** (OE *tige hamm,* goat field) is an abandoned village situated in an isolated valley, sheltered to the north by the Purbeck Hills and to the south by a steep limestone ridge.    As part of the MoD Lulworth Ranges it can only be visited when they are open.

There are fine panoramic views over the valley from the minor road that runs along the Purbeck Hills ridge. **Povington**

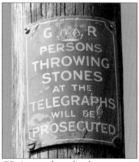

*GR sign on telegraph pole*

Hill (SY888811, 187m) overlooks Tyneham and most of the MoD ranges. This road is occasionally closed during live firing exercises.

Today the village has a feeling of sadness about it. With its old telephone box, brand new in 1929, and ruined houses, it has a feeling of derelict vandalism. The school and church have been repaired. The former is presented as it would have been in the 1930s, while the latter is a museum, telling the story of the parish.

**Paths**    There are numerous marked trails here. The Gwyle, the small wooded valley which follows a stream to the shore, has willows so spattered with shrapnel that they cannot be sawed down.    Hulks of old shot-up tanks litter the valley.

Circular walks can take in the whole area or much shorter distances. The coastal trail all the way to Kimmeridge is spectacular. **Tyneham Cap** (170m) had a radar station in WWII called RAF Brandy Bay. Little remains except some unsightly ruins today.

**Gad Cliff** (*gad*, steel wedge) reaches a height of 130m below **Tyneham Cap**. This dramatic wedge-shaped feature runs from an escarpment east of Worbarrow Tout all round Brandy Bay to the Long Ebb. The cliffs are mainly Portland Limestone, sloping upwards at about 50° and are capped with Purbeck Limestone.

**Brandy Bay** was a favoured place for smugglers to land their illicit goods and spirit them inland. With few houses

*Tyneham Village*

*Tyneham School*

*Worbarrow Bay on left, Tyneham Village in centre and Povington Hill on the right*

or roads, this area was ideal for clandestine operations.

**Broad Bench and Long Ebb** are areas of hard limestone which are revealed at low tide. During storms impressive seas break here. There are dramatic views of Gad Cliff over Holbarrow Bay from the headland above Charnel. When the light is right the jaggy cliffs reveal the source of their name.

*1929 telephone box*

*Gad Cliff looking west from near Tyneham Cap*

*Gad Cliff looking east from Tyneham Cap*

## TYNEHAM

This sleepy valley was requisitioned by the MoD in late 1943 for use as an extension to the Lulworth Ranges during the lead-up to D-Day.

All 205 residents were evacuated from the parish, never to return. They left a message on the church door, which reads, *"Please treat the church and houses with care; we have given up our homes where many of us lived for generations to help win the war to keep men free. We shall return one day and thank you for treating the village kindly."*

The Bond family, who had owned the valley for over 500 years, were assured that the estate would be returned to them after the war. However this was not to be as the government bought the parish of Tyneham in 1947 by compulsory purchase.

Tyneham House had been used by the RAF for staff from the radar station on Tyneham Cap. Built in the 1560s, this fine old house was torn down in 1967 by the Ministry of Works. Now called English Heritage, this government body is normally tasked with the care of ancient sites and old buildings.

For over six decades attempts have been made to get the area released from MoD control, including a parliamentary enquiry which recommended the range be closed. This was overturned, but in 1975 limited public access was agreed. Over seventy years from D-Day, many would view the Army's continued presence here as inappropriate and that the time has come to clean it up and leave. Dorset Wildlife Trust would be an appropriate owner.

# KIMMERIDGE

*The jagged buttresses of Gad Cliff overlook Kimmeridge Bay*

**KIMMERIDGE BAY** (OE *cyme ric*, handy small road) has low cliffs, composed of Jurassic clays, shales and harder cementstone. The Kimmeridge Clay Formation is famous for the diversity of fossils, which include Ammonites, Ichthyosaurs, Plesiosaurs and numerous fish species.

**The Flats** are areas of hard limestone which are resistant to erosion by the sea. To the east are The Ledges, while Broad Bench is only accessible when the MoD ranges are open. At low tide a large area of rocks and rock pools is exposed, making this an ideal place to study shore life and search for fossils. A snorkel trail encourages exploration.

**Oil Shale,** Blackstone or "Kimmeridge Coal", occurs in

*"Nodding Donkey" extracting oil*

the cliffs. This bituminous, soft rock has been used for thousands of years to make jewellery and decorative objects as it is easily carved, or turned on a hand lathe. It occasionally self-ignites when newly exposed due to the presence of iron pyrites and burns brightly, giving off a strong smell of sulphur.

Over the centuries many people have sought to get rich by exploiting this Jurassic shale. The manufacture of alum, salt and glass were tried. Oil and tar were extracted, gas was distilled and numerous other enterprises tried but nobody made much money. All such attempts did however produce a great deal of nasty smells.

**Oil Well** The "nodding donkey" on the west side of the bay is a beam pump which extracts oil from a reservoir 350m below ground. These Middle Jurassic rocks are the same strata from which much North Sea oil comes from. This was one of the first successful onshore wells in the UK, and has been in operation since 1959 but now only produces c.65 barrels per day (10,000l).

**Purbeck Marine Wildlife Reserve** extends from Bacon Hole on Mupe Bay in the west to St Aldhelm's Head in the east. The Fine Foundation Marine Centre on the east side of the bay has aquaria with examples of various local species. It is staffed by DWT marine wardens and includes interactive educational displays.

**Clavell Tower** was built by Rev. John Clavell of Smedmore House in the 1820s as a summerhouse. It was used by Coastguards until it went on fire in the 1930s. Now owned by the Landmark Trust, it was moved 25m inland and reopened in 2008 as a holiday let.

**Viewpoints** There are dramatic views to the west over Kimmeridge Bay from the approach road and from Hen

*Clavell Tower is a 19ᵗʰ century folly*

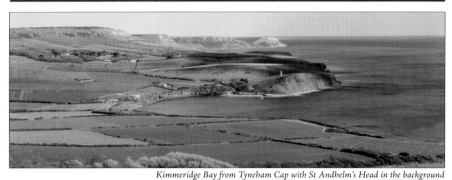

*Kimmeridge Bay from Tyneham Cap with St Andhelm's Head in the background*

Cliff next to Clavell Tower. The jagged Portland Limestone buttresses of Gad Cliff loom, saw-like, in the west.

**Nature** The tops and clay parts of the cliffs here have Rock Samphire, Wild Cabbage, Yellow-horned Poppy, Sea Kale, Sea Sandwort and Sea Rocket. Thrift, Sea Plantain, Red and Sea Campion add colour.

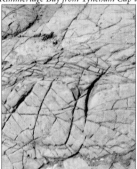

*The Flats*

*Shale, clay and cementstone strata*

### NEW FOSSIL MUSEUM

The Kimmeridge Fossil Museum is due to open in 2016 to house the Etches Collection of over 2,000 local Jurassic fossils. *"Engaging and interactive exhibitions supported by fieldwork projects and outreach programmes. The exhibition area will be constantly refreshed with new displays."*

*The Kimmeridge Ledges and Hen Cliff*

*Fine Foundation Marine Centre*

*Kimmeridge cliffs from the west*

# CHAPMAN'S POOL & ST ALDHELM'S HEAD

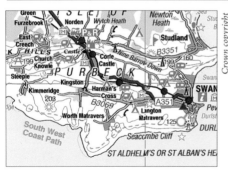

*Crown copyright*

*Looking south to St Aldhelm's Head from Emmett's Hill*

**The Southwest Coast Path** hugs undulating cliffs from Kimmeridge Bay to Durlston Head, except for an inland detour above Chapman's Pool.

**Swyre Head** (OE *swēora*, neck, narrow headland, 203m, SY933784), the highest elevation in the Isle of Purbeck, is c.800m inland from the coast up a steep incline. There is a wonderful panoramic view of most of Purbeck and far beyond. It can also be reached from parking areas near Kingston and Kimmeridge.

**Houns-tout Cliff**, west of Chapman's Pool is another fine viewpoint. From here the path goes inland to avoid a large landslide. There is a steep climb up over this 140m headland with its slumped cliffs overlooking Egmont Point.

**Chapman's Pool** is a delightful, little-frequented bay reached from near Renscombe Farm, west of Worth Matravers. The cliffs are formed from fossiliferous Kimmeridge Clay. Ammonites are easy to find on the shore here. The shed and slipway on the east side of the bay were built in 1866 for a new lifeboat station but this was abandoned in 1880 due to lack of a nearby crew.

**Emmetts Hill Memorial** commemorates all Royal Marines lost in action from 1945. It has a small memorial garden surrounded by a Purbeck Limestone wall and overlooks Chapman's Pool from the east.

**St Aldhelm's Head** (108m) is about 1,000m further south along the cliffs. The path descends steeply to sea level and

back up steps where it meets a deep valley. The headland is yet another superb viewpoint and has a lookout station.

**St Aldhelm's Chapel** is thought to date from Norman times, and may originally have been a lookout station for Corfe Castle. Its use as a chapel is first recorded in the 1260s. It is square , with a large central column supporting four vaults. The doorway and small window are Norman. The interior is about 8m across, while the corners point to the cardinal points of the compass. The chapel undoubtedly also served as a sea mark for mariners.

**WWII Radar Station** The headland was used by the Telecommunications Research Establishment at RAF Worth Matravers. There was

*Emmett's Hill Royal Marines' Memorial*

*St Aldhelm's Chapel interior*

Chapman's Pool and Houns-tout Cliff

also a Chain Home radar station here, part of the first national air defence radar system. There is a monument to those who worked on radar in WWII nearby.

**Winspit** (OE *wince pitt*, winch pit) is a small inlet about 1.5mi (2km) east of St Aldhelm's head. Here the cliffs are pock marked with quarry caves, where Portland Limestone was formerly extracted in huge quantities to be exported as building blocks. Today most are home to bats, many are fenced off, but some can be explored with a torch.

**Worth Matravers** (OE *worð*, enclosure) is an attractive little village just inland from Winspit. The Square and Compass pub dates from c.1776 and has an interesting

display of fossils. Limestone cottages surround an attractive pond. The Church of St Nicholas of Myra dates from the 12th century and, despite renovations, retains many original features.

**Smallpox** The graveyard is the last resting place of Benjamin and Elizabeth Jesty. The headstone states, "*To the Memory OF Benj.in. Jesty (of Downshay) who departed this Life, April 16th 1816 aged 79 Years. He was born at Yetminster in this County, and was an upright honest Man: particularly noted for having been the first Person (known) that Introduced the Cow Pox by Inoculation, and who from his great strength of mind made the Experiment from the (Cow) on his Wife and two Sons in the Year 1774*".

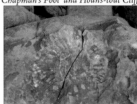
Ammonite fossil

WWII Radar Memorial

Old lifeboat shed and slipway

St Aldhelm's Chapel

Winspit from the east

Old Harry Rocks and Handfast Point

# Durlston Country Park

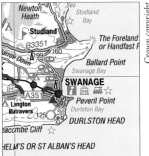

*Crown copyright*

*Anvil Point and Durlston Head from the east*

**Durlston Country Park** (OE *thyrelod stān*, from a now-fallen natural arch) is owned by Dorset County Council and covers 113ha. It is a National Nature Reserve, one of the prime destinations in Dorset for anyone interested in nature. It genuinely claims that, *"The wildlife at Durlston will keep an interested person busy for years and an expert for even longer."*

**Daily Diary and Events** The Park maintains a very useful Daily Diary on its website, durlston.co.uk, with details of sightings, weather, wild flowers, birds and insects. This is very helpful when planning a trip. Details of events are also available on the website.

**Waymarked Trails** start and finish at the castle. These include coastal, woodland, wildlife and Victorian heritage routes. The reserve is crisscrossed with paths, which traverse all its habitats.

**Durlston Castle** was built by George Burt, who bought the Cliff and Sentry Estate in 1862. He intended to develop a residential area here, but this did not come to fruition. The building was opened in 1891, complete with its 8m diameter Great Globe, carved stone inscriptions and London cast iron bollards.

The Castle was extensively renovated and reopened in 2011, as a Visitor Centre with interactive displays, an exhibition gallery, shop and restaurant. The Belvedere and roof terraces offer panoramic views.

**Flora** The calcareous downland here supports over 500 kinds of wildflowers, in particular an abundance of orchids. Of the six species here, the rare spring-flowering Ear-

*Early-spider Orchid*

*Lulworth Skipper*

*The Great Globe*

*Durlston Castle*

ly-spider Orchid is the most sought after by enthusiasts. It flowers in late April for only a few days.

The secret of Durlston's biodiversity is its range of habitats, ranging from cliffs, coastal grassland, unspoilt meadows, old hedges and scrubby woodland to dry-stone dykes. The area has never been intensively farmed, but was formerly heavily quarried for its exceptional Portland Limestone.

**Butterflies** At least 33 species of butterflies breed here. This is prime territory for the rare Lulworth Skipper, which depends on Tor Grass as its larval food plant. Common, Adonis and Chalk-hill Blues, as well as Dingy and Small Skippers are just a few others that can be observed here.

**Birds** Razorbill, Guillemot, Shag and Fulmar Petrel breed on the cliffs. Warblers such as Whitethroat, Blackcap and Chiffchaff nest in the hedges and scrub. Dartford Warbler, Stonechats, Bullfinches, Yellowhammer, Linnet, Skylark and a few Black Redstart also breed here.

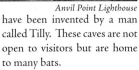
*Anvil Point Lighthouse*

It is during spring and autumn migration times that Durlston really comes into its own for birdwatchers. Huge numbers of Swallows and Sand Martins and other birds congregate here before moving south in autumn. In all, about 270 species of birds have been observed on the headland.

**Tilly Whim Caves** (OE *wimm*, windlass) are called after the cranes used to load blocks of stone onto boats below, said to have been invented by a man called Tilly. These caves are not open to visitors but are home to many bats.

**Anvil Point Lighthouse** was first lit in 1881. The light is 45m above mean high water and has a range of nine nautical miles. Now automatic, it was fitted with an LED lamp in 2012. The lighthouse was designed to be a waypoint to guide ships passing from Portland Bill to the Solent.

*Green-winged Orchid*

*Chalk Milkwort*

*Tilly Whim*

*Windlass and workings*

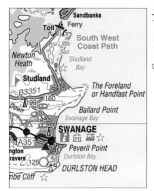

*Crown copyright*

*Swanage from Ballard Down*

**SWANAGE** (OE *swān wīc*, swain's dairy farm, popn. 2011, 10,124) is a pleasant seaside town, at the seaward end of an attractive valley which extends as far as Tyneham. This fertile area of Wealdon Beds and Greensand is sheltered by the Purbeck Hills to the north and the coastal Purbeck Limestone ridge to the south.

**Danish Shipwrecks** In 877AD the Anglo-Saxon Chronicle records a major loss of Danish ships here. This has been claimed as a great victory for King Alfred the Great, *"This year came the Danish army into Exeter from Wareham; whilst the navy sailed west about, until they met with a great mist at sea, and there perished one hundred and twenty ships at Swanwich."*

The probable explanation is that a Danish fleet was lost, but not by naval action. More likely is that they became disorientated in the fog and were caught in the tide, which bore them onto the shallow ledges off Peveril Point.

**Quarrying** has been important here since Roman times. They used Purbeck Marble to decorate the interiors of their buildings. Purbeck Limestone was extensively employed in construction. After the demise of Roman power, the industry went into decline until the Saxons and, later, the Normans commenced building grand stone churches, abbeys and cathedrals.

During the 17th century Purbeck Limestone was in great demand,

*Swanage from Peveril Point*

*Swanage seafront from an old postcard*

*The Town Hall has an older facade*

particularly during the rebuilding of London after the Great Fire of 1666. Its weather resistance and ease of working made it ideal for use as building stone and for pavements. Quarried stone was loaded onto lighters at Dancing Ledge, Winspit and other places, then ferried to Swanage Beach. There it was loaded onto ships for delivery to London and many other destinations.

*Swanage from the east*

**Swanage Steam Railway** The railway arrived in Swanage in 1885 which gave an immediate boost to an already thriving tourism industry. The present cast iron "new" pier dates from 1895 and was built to encourage passenger steamers. The railway branch line was closed by British Rail in 1972. Later that year, the Swanage Railway Society was set up and by 1995 there were regular services to Norden via Corfe Castle. In 2009 the first public Wareham to Swanage service was run by Virgin Trains. The Society hope to restart regular services to Wareham by 2015.

*Swanage Railway Station*

**Seaside Resort** Swanage is an attractive seaside resort with a sheltered, gently sloping beach of fine white sand. It has plenty of accommodation, restaurants, amusements and visitor services, yet remains unspoilt and low key. The town retains many features imported from London by Mowlems, including the 1872 Town Hall with its 1670 facade, the 1854 Wellington Clock re-erected here in 1866, street bollards with London names and, of course, its cast iron pier.

*George Burt*
*Wellington Clock and New Pier*

### GEORGE BURT

George Burt (1816-1894) was the nephew of John Mowlem, who founded the highly successful London building contractor firm, in 1822. The company undertook many major works and was a prodigious user of Purbeck stone. Burt took over in 1844 and further expanded the business. He retained a great interest in his home town and built waterworks, gasworks as well as several buildings. Parts of London buildings which were salvaged during development works were resited in Swanage. He built Purbeck House in High Street in the 1870s. Its walls consist of multicoloured marble offcuts left over from the Albert Memorial. This massive building is now a hotel and stands opposite the equally imposing Town Hall.

*Old Harry Rocks from the sea*

**Ballard Down** (SZ025812, 162m) forms the eastern end of the Purbeck Hills chalk ridge. It is also the easternmost point of the Jurassic Coast World Heritage Site. This extends westwards for 96mi (155km), to Orcombe Point near Exmouth.

Ballard Cliff is the scarp slope of the chalk ridge and forms the sloping north side of Swanage Bay. From Ballard Point, spectacular white vertical chalk cliffs, called Old Nick's Ground, end at the Foreland, or Handfast Point. The cliffs are best seen from the sea on a boat trip from Swanage. A few Puffins and Guillemots nest here.

**Old Harry Rocks** are a series of rock stacks which extend seawards from Handfast Point. The best view is perhaps from the ferry from Poole to Cherbourg, but they are spectacular from any angle. They are stumps of a chalk ridge that extended all the way to the Isle of Wight and Kent, which has been steadily eroded by the sea.

**Godlingston Manor** dates from the 14th century or earlier. Despite many alterations and a disastrous fire in 1871, it still retains its medieval round tower, very strongly built in solid Purbeck stone. The nearby brickworks have utilised the Wealdon clay and coarse quartz grit deposits here for hundreds of years.

**Viewpoints** Kingswood Down (109m, SZ006819) on the B3351 offers a fine view over the heathland NNR, Studland and Poole Harbour. A short, but a steep walk to the top of Godlingston Hill (200m, SZ008812) will reveal a superb 360° panorama of much of Purbeck.

**Studland** (OE *stōd land*, horse land) nestles under Ballard Down. Most of the buildings date from the 20th century, but the ancient **St Nicholas' Church** is one of the best in Dorset. It was originally built by the Saxons, in the early 11th century, before being greatly modified by the Normans in the late 12th century.

**The Agglestone** (OE *helig stān*, holy stone) or the Devil's Anvil is a large sandstone boulder which rests on a little hillock on the heath inland from Studland. Legend has it that the devil himself threw it here from the Isle of Wight.

*Guillemots on Ballard Cliff*

*Puffins nest on the cliffs below Old Nick's Ground*

He was apparently trying to hit Corfe Castle. Some say the name means "wobbly stone" as to *"aggle"* in Dorset means to wobble. In former times it could be moved on its perch, but slumped over in 1970.

**Studland Bay** has a 4mi (6km) sandy beach, stretching from Redend Point to South Haven Point. This very popular stretch of sands includes a naturist area and is backed by extensive dunes. The beach can be accessed from several carparks. **South Haven Point** marks the eastern end of the South West Coast Path and is also the southern terminal for the chain ferry to Sandbanks just across the entrance to Poole Harbour.

**Studland Visitor Centre** on Knoll Beach has information displays on the diverse habits and wildlife in the area and the story of the Jurassic Coast. There is also a cafe and many facilities for visitors. What is said to be the best naturist beach in the UK is about 800m along the beach from the car park. *"Amazing beach and secluded dunes - one of the best naturist beaches in Europe......if you have the weather!!!"*

*Studland Bay and NNR with part of Poole Harbour from Ballard Down*

**Studland and Godlingston Heath NNR** covers 631ha of heathland, sand dunes, peat bog, and shallow freshwater lagoons. Rare species here include the Dartford Warbler and Nightjar as well as all six species of native reptiles. It also holds many dragonflies and bees. In winter, large flocks of wildfowl and waders mass here. This reserve, as well as Ballard Down, is owned and managed by the National Trust, as part of the Bankes Kingston Lacy Estate bequest.

**WWII** Studland was extensively used for training and live firing exercises during the run up to D-Day. Churchill, King George VI, Montgomery, Eisenhower and other "top brass" watched practice landings from the safety of **Fort Henry** (SZ037828). Situated on Redend Point, this massive bunker formed part of the coast defences of the area, and is on the Studland Beach Second World War walk.

*Studland has four miles of sandy beaches*

*St Nicholas' Church in Studland dates from Saxon times*

*St Nicholas' Church interior*

# CORFE CASTLE

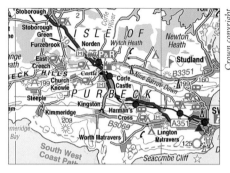

*Crown copyright*

*Tumbled towers*

*From East Hill*

**CORFE CASTLE** (OE *corfe*, pass or gap) is an unspoilt and very picturesque village, overlooked by one of the most impressive castles in the whole country. There was originally a Saxon fort on the top of this strategically important knoll in the middle of the pass, and doubtless an Iron Age one before it.

**Normans** The stone castle was started by William the

Conqueror, one of over 40 in England. These were mostly of wood, but Corfe Castle was partially built in Purbeck stone. By 1105, Henry I's keep was complete and over the centuries the castle was expanded. It withstood a siege by King Stephen's army in 1139 during the Anarchy Civil War.

Later, in 1244, Henry III had the keep limewashed. His

previous whitewashing of the Tower of London had been a great success. He was just continuing a much older fashion as the Romans are thought to have done the same with the north side of Hadrian's Wall.

By the 16<sup>th</sup> century, castles were becoming redundant due to the development of cannon, so Queen Elizabeth sold Corfe to her Lord Chancellor in 1572. It was then bought in 1635 by John Bankes, Charles I's Attorney General.

**Civil War** Lady Bankes held the castle with a tiny garrison until 1645, when the Parliamentarians managed to gain entry by deceit and took the fortress. Along with many others it was "slighted" by Act of Parliament. Gunpowder charges were placed, which succeeded in making the castle militarily useless. They also created one of the most atmospheric and romantic ruined castles in the UK.

**Visit** Corfe Castle is owned and operated by the National Trust. The ruins have been consolidated and repaired so that today it is one of the most

*The Castle from the entrance bridge*

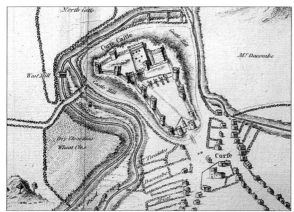

*Corfe Castle plan from 1586*

visited sites in Dorset. The ruins can be explored at leisure. Perhaps the best parts are the gatehouse, tumbled towers and the massive keep. The Trust have an interesting shop and cafe in the village.

**Events** Living history re-enactments by people in period dress, mock battles, Medieval cookery lessons and falconry displays are some of the activity on offer. Open air theatre includes Shakespeare plays. Children are well catered for with family trails and hands-on activities.

**Viewpoints** The best viewpoints over Corfe Castle are probably from the Purbeck Ridge. East Hill (103m), which is reached by a steep path below the castle, and West Hill (103m) both offer panoramic views over the castle, village and Purbeck. Early morning with mist and evening light are especially evocative.

**Walks** A great variety of circular walks along paths and quiet lanes can be undertaken from Corfe Castle, which makes an excellent centre. The only real downside is the continued lack of a bypass. Heavy traffic thunders through the village on the A351 to Swanage and the chain ferry to Poole. Care needs to be taken whilst enjoying the charms of the village.

### EDWARD THE MARTYR

After the death of Saxon King Edgar in 975 his eldest son, Edward, briefly succeeded him. He was murdered in March 978 at Corfe Castle, whilst visiting his step-mother Ælfthryth and half-brother Æthelred. He was buried without ceremony at Wareham. He may have been killed on the instigation of the step-mother, but there is no substantive evidence.

The Anglo-Saxon Chronicle recorded, *"No worse deed for the English race was done than this was, since they first sought out the land of Britain. Men murdered him, but God exalted him. In life he was an earthly king; after death he is now a heavenly saint. His earthly relatives would not avenge him, but his Heavenly Father has much avenged him."*

In 980 Edward's "incorrupt" body was transferred with great pomp to Shaftesbury. Although never canonised, he was popularly considered a saint and as a result the Abbey had many pilgrims. The Eastern Orthodox and Roman Catholic Churches consider him as a saint. Bones found in 1931, currently in the St Edward the Martyr Church in Brookword, Surrey, may perhaps be his.

Æthelred went on to become famous as *The Unready* (OE *unræd*, badly advised), during whose time attacks by the Danes became intense. He paid vast sums in *Danegeld* to buy them off. It was he who ordered the St Bride's Day massacre in 1002, when all Danes in England were to be executed. By late 1016 the Danes had effectively conquered the whole of England and Cnut was declared king.

*19th century photograph of Corfe Castle*

*Corfe Castle from East Hill*

**CORFE CASTLE VILLAGE** is a charming little place, marred only by the failure of the Dorset County Council to by-pass its centre. The houses are nearly all built of various types of Purbeck stone. Walls, roofs, street paving and lintels all use different types of limestone.

**Stone Trade** Corfe was, for centuries, prosperous because of the Purbeck Limestone and Marble quarried in the vicinity.

*The Free Arms*

The "marble" is in fact not genuine marble, which has been metamorphosed by adjacent volcanic activity. Instead it is a hard limestone containing many shells that polishes up very well. Unlike real marble it is not weather-resistant and thus only suitable for internal decoration, especially in churches.

Apart from building stone, a major product here was the capstones used to support grain stores. They were designed to prevent the incursion of rats and mice. Many of the buildings in the village date from the 16th century, including its oldest and smallest pub, the Free Arms, from 1568. The Greyhound Hotel in the Square has a porch dated 1733 and most older buildings are of a similar age.

**The Town Hall** is said to be the smallest in England. It was rebuilt after a fire in 1680, with the upper storey in brick and a stone roof. Downstairs there is a tiny, but interesting museum, which exhibits a small fraction of the artefacts and archives held. Upstairs the Meeting Room can accommodate up to 25 people.

**Corfe Castle Model Village** sets out to demonstrate what the castle and village would have looked like before the Civil War. There are games for all ages, a croquet lawn, fossils, a fairy garden and a shop with a tea room. Lost children are said *"to be sold off each Thursday at Wareham Market".*

**Swanage Railway** Corfe Castle is one of the stations on the heritage line from Norden to Swanage. Some services now go as far as Wareham. Dorset County Council bought the railway track bed with the intention of building a road bypass for the village but this did not happen. Corfe Castle station incorporates a small Railway Museum in a former goods shed.

*Marbler's Shoes and Football in the museum*

*Corfe Town Hall*

*The Square and the Greyhound Hotel*

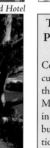

*Shrove Tuesday Football*

*The Blue Pool*

**The Blue Pool** (SY934834 ) is a former ball clay pit, first opened to the public in 1935. It is situated off the A351 northwest of Corfe Castle near Furzebrook. This area has been the centre of the clay industry for thousands of years, and remains so. The colours change depending on the light and time of day due to particles suspended in the clear water. There is a teahouse, museum, gift shop and plant centre. It is surrounded by a 10ha woodland nature reserve.

*Ticket office*

*Corfe Castle Station*

### THE ANCIENT ORDER OF PURBECK MARBLERS AND STONECUTTERS

Corfe annually hosts an ancient custom on Shrove Tuesday when the Ancient Order of Purbeck Marblers and Stonecutters meet in the Town Hall. Part of the business is to consider the induction of new apprentices.

Those aspiring to become freemen of the Order wait in the nearby Fox Inn, the oldest in Corfe. Those accepted for membership have to take a quart of ale, a loaf of bread and 6/8[d] (33p) to pay their dues.

Formerly a game of mass football was played for 3mi (4km) along a track over Rempstone Heath to Ower Quay, where a pound of pepper was paid to the land owner. Purbeck Stone and Marble were exported from this ancient pier for hundreds of years, before the railway arrived.

Today a game is still held in the village, but only in the streets. The farmer from Owen Farm now comes to collect his "peppercorn rent". Such games of mass football date from at least the 11th century and used to be common. Today the custom is still surprisingly widespread in the North of England and the Borders as well as in Cornwall and Kirkwall in Orkney.

*Corfe Castle from Kingston*

*The Scott Arms porch*

**INLAND VILLAGES** There is a series of highly attractive small villages south of the Purbeck Hills, south of Corfe Castle. These include Kingston and Worth Matravers to the south and Langton Matravers to the east. Church Knowle, Steeple and Kimmeridge lie to the west.

**Kingston**, situated 130m up on a ridge has fine views over

Corfe Common to Corfe Castle. Its very attractive stone cottages are somewhat overwhelmed by a large and ornate 19th century church, but this has not stopped the village being a popular film set. However the main attraction is the Scott Arms pub with its extensive menu and excellent views.

**Langton Matravers** (OE *lang tūn*, long settlement) has a

small, but interesting, museum, housed in a former coach house. It tells the story of the Purbeck stone industry with tools, worked stone, old photos and reconstructed underground quarry workings.

**Worth Matravers** (OE *worð*, enclosure) is a very picturesque Purbeck Stone village, with a large duckpond, inland from St Aldhelm's Head and Winspit. Its 12th century Norman church is one of the oldest in Dorset. The graveyard holds the headstones of Benjamin Jesty and his wife, Elizabeth Notley. Jesty was a pioneer of inoculation as a means of protection from smallpox.

For many, its unique pub, the Square and Compass, is the highlight. Few other pubs dou-

*The Square and Compass, Worth Matravers*

*Benjamin and Elizabeth Jesty's headstones*

*Langton Matravers Museum*

*Panoramic view north from East Hill, Corfe Castle*

ble up as a fossil and antiquarian museum. Ichthyosaurs, Plesiosaurs and Ammonites rub shoulders with Mesolithic, Neolithic, Bronze Age and Roman artefacts. This is an excellent starting point for circular walks in the area.

**Church Knowle** (OE, *cnoll*, small hill) is another pretty village with a fine 13th century Norman church. The cosy New Inn uses local meat and seafood for their traditional English pub food.

**Steeple** (OE *stēap hyll*, steep hill) is a tiny village sheltering below the highest point of the Purbeck Ridge (198m), best known for its connection with the first US president, George Washington. A stone panel and a ceiling panel in the church feature the coat of arms of Edward Lawrence, deceased in 1616. In 1390, Edmund Lawrence had married Agnes de Wessington; the inaugural President was a descendant and took this device for his signet ring and as the basis of the design of the flag for the fledgling United States of America - the Stars and Stripes.

*Steeple Church*

*Lawrence coat of arms*

*Lawrence coat of arms on ceiling*

### BENJAMIN JESTY

Benjamin Jesty had taken up the tenancy of Downshay Farm in c.1797, having previously farmed near Yetminster. Along with others he had experimented successfully with inoculation by cowpox as protection against the much more dangerous smallpox in the 1770s.

His headstone reads, "(Sacred) To the Memory OF Benj.in. Jesty (of Downshay) who departed this Life, April 16th 1816 aged 79 Years. He was born at Yetminster in this County, and was an upright honest Man: particularly noted for having been the first Person (known) that Introduced the Cow Pox by Inoculation, and who from his great strength of mind made the Experiment from the (Cow) on his Wife and two Sons in the Year 1774."

Wareham Saxon Walls overlook the floodplain of the River Piddle

# WAREHAM

*Crown copyright*

The Town Walls

**WAREHAM** (OE *wær hām*, Weir Farm, popn. 2011, 5,496) is strategically situated on a low promontory between the Rivers Frome and Piddle. It is protected from the north, east and south by the two rivers and their extensive, marshy flood plains. The River Frome is navigable from Poole Harbour via the Wareham Channel by shallow-draughted craft as far as Wareham Quay.

**Archaeology** Extensive excavations at **Bestwall** east of

*The Bull Hotel*

Boats at Wareham Quay

the town, have revealed the presence of Mesolithic people c.9000BC. Neolithic pottery, flints and axeheads dated to 3700BC, as well as a large settlement of Bronze Age round houses, were found. Excavations of the town walls have revealed much Iron Age and Roman pottery as well as coins and rubble.

**Saxon Walls** During the time of Alfred the Great, who was King of Wessex AD971-899, the kingdom was increasingly threatened by attacks from the Danes. They had even occupied Wareham during the winter of 876. In response he established a chain of fortified *burgs*, which included Wareham, Bridport, Christchurch, and Shaftesbury in Dorset.

The Town Walls remain impressive at over 4m high, sur-

rounded by a ditch nearly 4m deep in places. They enclose the town from the west, north and east, with the river to the south. Originally the Saxons built an earthen rampart revetted with timber supports and a palisade. Later, a stone wall and walkway was built on top. The defences enclose 34ha and the grid layout of the town still reflects the Saxon street plan.

**St Martin's Church**, near the north wall gate, mostly dates from the early 11th century and is the most complete Saxon church in Dorset. It is said to have been renovated by King Cnut during his reign c.1030, having been founded by St Aldhem in the 7th century. Despite repairs and additions over the centuries it retains much of its original features. This is perhaps because it is small and on the edge of town.

There are many wall paintings of various ages, the oldest being in the chancel, telling the story of St Martin, the famous 4th century French convert to Christianity. The north aisle is filled by a very large effigy of TE Lawrence of Arabia,

by Eric Kennington. Having originally been destined for Salisbury Cathedral, it seems out of place here. Perhaps it should be in Moreton Church, where his grave is and where his family connections were.

**History** The Normans built a castle here, but nothing now remains of this. Poole developed as a deep water port, ships became bigger and by the 14th century, the tidal approach to Wareham was too shallow for sea-going vessels. However it continued in commercial use, shipping out Purbeck stone and ball clay until the coming of the railway in 1847.

*Wareham Quay and the River Frome from the south bank*

*South Street from the Quay Square*

The town was hotly contested by the Parliamentarians and Royalists in the Civil War and narrowly escaped destruction. In 1762 much of Wareham was burnt down in a serious fire. It was rebuilt in Georgian style on the original town plan using brick and Purbeck limestone. Today the town retains its character, mostly unspoilt by 20th century developments.

**Wareham Today** The Quay, with its old stonework, wooden piles and open square is one of the most attractive parts of the town. The 17th century South Bridge and the south bank of the River Frome afford fine views.

North Bridge is older, but busier as it carries the main road into town from the north. Some of the more interesting buildings are the Rex, a cinema since 1920, the Red Lion and the Black Bear Hotel. The fine old Priory is now a hotel with lovely gardens leading down to the river.

The Museum in the Town Hall has displays on local archaeology, geology, military history and some fascinating TE Lawrence memorabilia.

*The Rex Cinema*

*St Martin's Church interior*

*St Martin's Church is on the Town Wall*

*Middlebere Lake from the Coombe Trail*

**ARNE RSPB RESERVE** (OE *ærn*, building, (SY971876, 563ha) opened in 1966. It includes lowland heath, old oak forest, grassland, reedbeds, saltmarsh and mud flats. Arne is a top class nature reserve, and an essential visit for wildlife enthusiasts at any time of year. It is situated about 4mi (6km) east of Wareham off the B3075 in Stoborough.

**The Visitor Centre** is the place to become orientated and pick up leaflets about the reserve. The RSPB hold many events here during the year, ranging from guided walks to Nightjar evenings and reptile weekends. Arne is a place that always has something new to see, regardless of the season, or weather.

**The Shipstal Point Trails** cover about 4mi (6.5km) of varied habitats. There is a hide overlooking Poole harbour and a fine beach with wonderful panoramic views.

**Coombe Heath Trail** passes a big pond before taking a large loop past a viewpoint and hide overlooking Middlebere Lake. The pond has Raft Spiders and dragonflies, while the heathland is the place for Dartford Warblers. The trail is about 1mi (1.5km).

**Arne in WWII** There was a battery of 4 heavy anti-aircraft guns (4.7in HAA) on Arne Hill during WWII. Its purpose was to defend the huge cordite factory at nearby Holton Heath. The peninsula was also used as a "Starfish" decoy. Large fires were lit on the heath during air raids to fool German bombers into dropping their bombs harmlessly in the countryside, rather than their proper targets.

Hundreds of bombs exploded here, peppering the area with

*Coombe Heath Pond*

*St Nicholas Church is 13ᵗʰ century*

*St Nicholas Church interior*

craters, but without damage to property or people. Suddenly there were large numbers of ponds which are highly suitable for the 22 species of dragonflies which may be seen here as well as Raft Spiders and many other insects.

**St Nicholas Church** dates from the 13th century and still has its original lancet windows. There are vestiges of wall paintings above the door. The inside is plain with whitewashed walls and 19th century fittings. There is no electricity so the lighting is by candles.

*Steve Round*
*Dartford Warbler*

*Steve Round*
*Hobby*

*Avocet*

*Durzan cirano*
*Nightjar*

*Steve Round*
*Black Darter*

*Sika Deer may be seen at Arne*

*Raft Spider*

*Dorset Heath*

*Middlebere Lake*

### ARNE STAR SPECIES

#### ALL YEAR
Dartford Warbler
Stonechat

#### SUMMER
Nightjar
Woodlark
Hobby
Peregrine
Marsh Harrier
Reptiles
Dorset Heath
Dragonflies
Raft Spider

#### MIGRATION TIMES
Osprey
Warblers
Whimbrel
Greenshank
Spoonbill

#### WINTER
Avocet
Black-tailed Godwit
Spoonbill
Brent Goose
Waterfowl
Gorse in flower
Hen Harrier
Merlin

*Poole Harbour and Poole from Brownsea Island*

**BROWNSEA ISLAND** (OE *Brūnocs ēg*, Brunoc's Isle, 202ha), is the largest in Poole Harbour. This tranquil, somewhat mystical place is an essential visit for anyone even slightly interested in nature. It can be reached from Poole Quay or Sandbanks by ferry. It has been owned by the National Trust since 1962; Dorset Wildlife Trust maintains the northern side as a nature reserve.

Brownsea Castle was first built as a blockhouse in 1547 to defend Poole Harbour, as part of Henry VIII's coastal defence strategy. Prior to the Dissolution, the island had belonged to Cerne Abbey since the 9th century. Since then it has belonged to a succession of people, some colourful, others reclusive. None ever made their fortune from it, while many spent a great deal of money.

The National Trust has a visitor centre, shop and cafe near the pier. Brownsea Castle and its surrounds is leased to the John Lewis Partnership for the use of their staff. With no roads or cars, the island is a haven of peace and quiet. It consists of oak and pine woods, heathland and saltmarsh with low cliffs and sandy beaches.

**Scouting** Robert Baden-Powell had his first encampment for boys on Brownsea Island in 1907. This led to his 1908 book *"Scouting for Boys"*, and the start of the hugely successful Scout Movement. In 1963 a permanent 20ha site was opened by Lady Baden-Powell for Scouts and Guides. Today a memorial to the first camp overlooks the purpose-built Baden-Powell Outdoor Centre, which has a shop, museum and facilities for the many Scouts and Guides who come to camp here annually.

**Red Squirrels** With its lack of development and highly varied habitats, the island is home to a great variety of species, some resident, others migratory. It is famous for its population of

*Brownsea Castle and dock*

*Landing on Brownsea Island*

*Woodland in the Dorset Wildlife Trust Reserve*

*Sandwich Terns breed here*

*Avocets overwinter in large numbers*

about 200 Red Squirrels, one of very few localities where they are still present in the south of England. Autumn is the best time to see them. Grey Squirrels have never been introduced here. Sika Deer are also present but are a continual nuisance as they prevent woodland regeneration. Fences have been erected to control them.

**Birds** The Lagoon, enclosed by a sea wall in the mid-19th century, is brackish and shallow, with a muddy bottom. Its level is controlled by a powerful automatic electric pump, making it ideal for wintering waders and safe for breeding terns. Five hides offer excellent views over the lagoon and reedbeds. The 101ha DWT Reserve also includes pinewoods, wet woodland, reedbeds, Alder carr, ponds and sandy beaches.

**Winter** In winter up to 1,500 Avocets make it their home, along with Black-tailed Godwit, Dunlin, Oyster Catcher, Curlew, Greenshank, Redshank, Grey Plover and other waders. Many waterfowl visit on migration or overwinter. Special trips visit the island sometimes during the winter.

**Summer** There are large colonies of Common and Sandwich Terns as well as gulls. Little Egrets, Grey Heron, Kingfishers, Water Rails, Reed Warblers, Little Grebe Shelduck and Tufted Duck all breed here. There is a thriving population of Water Voles. They may frequently be seen from the hides and along the waterways.

*Baden-Powell and boys at first camp*

*Scouts' first camp monument*

*Peacock*

*Red Squirrel*

*Laurie Campbell*

*Sand cliffs on the southwest side*

*Corfe Castle in early morning from East Hill*

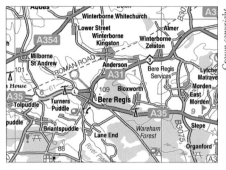

*Crown copyright*

*St John the Baptist Church, Bere Regis*

**NORTH PURBECK** The border of the Isle of Purbeck was formerly the River Frome. The northern border of the current administrative district more or less follows the A31 from west of Bere Regis to Corfe Mullen , west of Poole.

**Bere Regis** (B *bāer*, woodland pasture) was rebuilt in brick after a devastating fire in 1788, which gives it a coherent, pleasant old fashioned feel. The busy A31 and A35 main roads, bypass Bere Regis, from which it benefits greatly. The St John

the Baptist Church fortunately survived all the conflagrations. It dates originally from the 11th century and has considerable stonework visible from the 12th and 13th centuries. Despite additions and repairs over the years it retains a pleasing building.

It is chiefly known for its highly ornate nave roof, said to have been financed by John Morton, along with the church tower. Five large beams, together with a complex system of timbers, are richly decorated with many multicoloured carvings. Most dramatic are the figures of the 12 apostles, sticking out and looking down on the nave, each identifiable by his dress and possessions.

John Morton was born in nearby Milborne St Andrew, and rose to became first Archbishop of Canterbury and then

*15th century nave roof in St John the Baptist Church, Bere Regis*

*Toothache*

*Headache*

*Norman font*

Lord Chancellor in 1487 under Henry VI. He is credited with what we would now call paying off the deficit by means of his sound fiscal policies. "Morton's Fork" was a dilemma for the rich, "*If the subject is seen to live frugally, tell him because he is clearly a money saver of great ability, he can afford to give generously to the King. If, however, the subject lives a life of great extravagance, tell him he, too, can afford to give largely, the proof of his opulence being evident in his expenditure.*"

**Shitterton** (OE *scitere tūn*, Shitter Farm, since its stream was used as the sewer) is over the Bere River from Bere Regis. This protected it from the many fires which its larger neighbour suffered. As a result it is a very attractive little village with many old, thatched buildings. These include 550-year old Honeycombe Cottage, now a B&B.

Due to its name, the village was constantly losing its signpost. The community got together and bought a 1.5tonne block with the name carved into it. One of the inhabitants commented, "*Let's put in a ton and a half of stone and see them try and take that away in the back of a Ford Fiesta*".

**Woodbury Hill** (SY857948)is an Iron Age hillfort just east of Bere Regis. A famous fair was held here for five days over the autumn equinox, from at least the 12th century. Traders, dealers, farmers, entertainers and

*St John the Baptist Church, Bere Regis*

large numbers of the public came from far and wide. By the early 20th century it had declined to two days and despite attempts at revival, after WWII, ended in 1951.

**Charborough House** is surrounded by a high brick wall, which is passed by the A31. The Stag (SY920993) and Lion Gates celebrate the diversion of the turnpike road in 1841. The house is famous for

being the venue for the meeting in 1686, which set in motion the Glorious Revolution of 1688, in which James II was deposed. William of Orange and his wife Mary Stuart were appointed King and Queen.

The host was Thomas Erle, MP of Wareham, an ancestor of the present Richard Drax, current MP for South Dorset. Charborough Park is occasionally open to the public.

*Honeycombe Cottage in Shitterton is over 550 years old*

*Charborough House from an old print*

# The Tank Museum, Bovington

*Mark I tank in early camouflage*

**Bovington Camp** (OE Bōfa -ingtūn, Bofa's farm, SY829884), is a large British Army base situated north of Wool. The War Office had bought 25ha of land here in 1899 to be used as a "rifle range or for any other military use or purpose." In 1916, what was to become the Tank Corps moved here. The camp, along with Lulworth Ranges, remains the central training base for British Army fighting vehicles.

**The Tank Museum** was initially proposed by Rudyard Kipling, during a visit in 1923, when he looked at a forlorn array of WWI tanks. Luckily the army had the foresight to retain a representative selection of them over the years. The Museum opened to the public in 1947 and has since expanded into one of the largest of its kind in the world.

The exhibitions cover the development and history of tanks over nearly a century. Displays include WWI, developments between the wars, WWII, the Cold War and recent conflicts. The Vehicle Conservation Centre was added in 2013 to house over 100 additional military vehicles, in addition to nearly 300 tanks from about 26 countries.

**Special Events** Many of the tanks in the museum are in full working order. The Tank Museum Experience Day *"offers the chance to ride in a Main Battle Tank, learn to drive an armoured personnel vehicle"*. The Access All Areas Experience is a behind the scenes visit. Both include an in depth guided tour of the museum.

**Famous Tanks** include early WWI machines. The restored WWII German Tiger I is another of the star attractions. Also among the WWII exhibits are the main protagonists from the Allied, German and Russian sides. These include the M4 Sherman, Panzers, Panthers and the most-produced tank of all, the T-34. The German tanks may have been the best, but the ability of the Allies to vastly outproduce them was to be crucial.

**WWI Prototypes** *Little Willie* is one of the centrepieces of the Tank Museum's collection. This first prototype was built by Foster & Co in 1915 to meet the requirement of the Landships Committee for a war engine capable of crossing a trench 1.5m wide. It utilised parts from existing vehicles, especially the Foster-Daimler gun tractor.

This prototype was to influence the design of all future tanks. It led to the development of the Mark I tank, a code word which stuck. These machines were rhombus-shaped, with tracks which went all around the hull. To keep the centre of gravity low, the armament was mounted in side sponsons.

*M4 Sherman "Firefly" with 76mm gun*

*Russian T-34 and a burning German Tiger*

*Mark IV Tank*

*The interior was undivided, noisy and full of fumes*

They were designed to climb parapets over 1m high, cross trenches 2.5m wide, shell holes and to crush barbed wire.

**First Actions** Orders for 150 machines were placed in February 1916. They were first used at the Battle of the Somme in September 1916, and in small numbers in other battles. The first major use was at the Battle of Amiens in August 1918, when c.580 tanks took part in a major offensive. Only six remained operational after four days, but armoured support had proven crucial to breaking through the German lines.

The introduction of the tank proved to be a critical juncture on the Western Front. After the battle, Philip Gibbs, a war correspondent, wrote *"The initiative of attack is so completely in our hands that we are able to*

*Centurion Tank cut in half*

*strike him at many different places. The change has been greater in the minds of men than in the taking of territory. On our side the army seems to be buoyed up with the enormous hope of getting on with this business quickly, but there is a change also in the enemy's mind. They no longer have even a dim hope of victory on this western front. All they hope for now is to defend themselves long enough to gain peace by negotiation."*

This epitomises what might be called the British way of doing things. After almost four years of unremitting trench warfare, a completely new weapon which had been developed from scratch, transformed land warfare for at least the next century. This was not thought up by any of the top generals or their staff, none of whom knew how to end the war.

*German Tiger I*

It had depended on the genius of Winston Churchill and the lateral thinking of a few military people, combined with the common sense and imaginativeness of an agricultural machinery manufacturer in Lincolnshire. The early tanks may have been unreliable, vulnerable, dangerous for their crews and somewhat Heath Robinson, but they were also a game changer.

*Little Willie*

*TE Lawrence in Arab dress*

**TE Lawrence**, or *"Lawrence of Arabia"* remains an enigmatic and charismatic character, very much of his time. He inhabited the shadowy world of intelligence, guerrilla war and supplying arms. He played key roles in the "Great Game" of the Middle East during and after WWI. The impression is that there is more to the story than has been published.

*"Seven Pillars of Wisdom"*, Lawrence's memoir of his wartime exploits is his main literary work. First published as an expensive private edition, it remains in print today. The title is from *Proverbs, 9,1*, *"Wisdom hath builded her house, she hath hewn out her seven pillars"*. An abridged version, *"Revolt in the Desert"* was published in 1927 and was a resounding success.

**Clouds Hill** (SY823909) is a little cottage about 1.5mi (2.5km) north of the Bovington Camp and the Tank Museum. Lawrence rented this dilapidated cottage in 1923 from his cousins, the Framptons, owners of the Moreton Estate, during his time at Bovington Camp. In 1925 he bought and renovated the building, which he intended to retire to in 1935 when his term in the RAF was finished. Sadly he had an accident that year with his Brough Superior motorbike near the cottage. He died from head injuries 6 days after the crash.

Of it he said, *"Nothing in Clouds Hill is to be a care upon the world. While I have it there shall be nothing exquisite or unique in it. Nothing to anchor me."* In fact it very clearly was his sanctuary, where he had peace to write and escape. He also entertained many famous literary figures here.

Clouds Hill belongs to the National Trust, which maintains it as it was before Lawrence's death. The main upstairs Music Room was where he wrote, listened to music and entertained friends. Downstairs, the Book Room was where he kept his impressive library. Many of his books were personally signed by famous authors. Unfortunately they were all sold on his death.

**Moreton** (OE mōr tūn, Moor Farm) is a pretty little village southwest of Clouds Hill, about 3mi (5km) by road. It can also be reached by following the Lawrence of Arabia Trail by walking through Moreton Plantation 2mi (3km). Lawrence is buried

*Lawrence on his Brough Superior motorbike*

*Effigy in St Martin's Church, Wareham*

*The Music Room, Clouds Hill*

in the cemetery. His funeral was attended by many famous people including Winston and Clementine Churchill.

St Nicholas Church in Moreton was completed in 1776, in Georgian Gothic style, to replace a previous one that dated from at least the 13th century. In October 1940 a lone German bomb fell nearby and causing considerable damage, including smashing the windows. This was a blessing in disguise as the highly impressive new windows are engraved by Laurence Whistler. These alone make St Nicholas worth visiting even for those not usually drawn to churches.

**Wareham** There is a large effigy of Lawrence in the aisle of St Martin's Church, created by Eric Kennington. He is in Arab dress with his head on a

camel saddle. The Wareham Town Museum has documents and artefacts relating to Lawrence in a special display.

*Lawrence's grave in Moreton*

*One of the Whistler windows*

*Moreton church has fine engraved windows by Whistler*

### TE LAWRENCE 1888-1935

Thomas Edward Lawrence graduated from Oxford University in 1910 with a first in modern history. He was already interested in the Middle East, having done a thesis on Crusader fortifications. From 1911 to 1914, he worked on British Museum archaeological excavations, mainly at Carchemish in Syria.

Fluent in Arabic, he had also travelled widely in Mesopotamia and the Levant. In October 1914 he was commissioned and sent to Egypt as an intelligence officer. Britain was planning to instigate and finance an Arab revolt against the Ottoman Empire. Lawrence was instrumental as a liaison officer in persuading key Arabs to cooperate with the British. The culmination was the fall of Damascus in September 1918.

One officer is quoted as saying, *"Though a price of £15,000 has been put on his head by the Turks, no Arab has, as yet, attempted to betray him. The Sharif of Mecca has given him the status of one of his sons, and he is just the finely tempered steel that supports the whole structure of our influence in Arabia. He is a very inspiring gentleman adventurer."*

Lawrence ended the war as a colonel and continued to work for the Foreign Office. He attended the Paris Peace Conference on behalf of the Arabs. He was also an advisor on the staff of Winston Churchill, then Secretary of State at the Colonial Office in 1921-22. At the Cairo Conference he was instrumental in gaining independence for Jordan and Iraq. Between 1922 and 1935 he served in the RAF, with a short time in the Army.

# Nature, Art, Monkeys & Nuclear Energy

*Woolbridge Manor House and the River Frome*

*Silver-studded Blue male*

**WEST PURBECK** is home to an eclectic mixture of interesting sites. World class nature reserves, modern art, rescued monkeys and even nuclear power all feature.

**Heathland Nature Reserves** include Higher Hyde (see opposite) as well as Tadnoll & Winfrith Heaths. These fragments of a habitat that once covered most of this area host a large range of plants, insects, reptiles and birds. There is something to see at all seasons, but late summer is the best time for colour as the heather blooms. Spring is best for many birds, while in July the butterflies and dragonflies are at their most abundant.

**Wool** (OE *wella*, The Springs) is a small village on the River Stour with a very pretty old bridge, which may date from the 16th century. A bridge existed here in 1343 and most likely long before that. Woolbridge Manor House is Elizabethan and belonged to the Turbeville family for many years. It is said that a phantom coach and horses may be seen crossing the bridge on dark and stormy nights.

**Monkey World Centre** (65ha, SY846884) is 1mi (1.5km) north of Wool. It was founded in 1987 by Jim Cronin to house Chimpanzees rescued from Spanish beaches. It *"assists governments around the world to stop the smuggling of primates from the wild."*

Refugees of illegal trading as well as apes that have been abused or neglected are re-

*Higher Hyde Heath Nature Reserve*

*Monkey World Centre*

*Monkey World Centre*

*Silver-studded Blue male*

*Keeled Skimmer female*

Higher Hyde Heath (54ha, SY 854899) is a DWT reserve on the Puddletown Road east of Bovington Camp. It comprises dry and wet heath, damp woodland and old gravel pits. For the sheer variety of wildlife to be seen throughout the year it has to be one of the best reserves in Dorset. All six British reptiles are present.

Rare birds include Dartford Warbler and Woodlark but the huge variety of butterflies and dragonflies is perhaps the biggest feature, with July possibly the best month to visit. Silver-studded Blue butterflies are perhaps the stars of a large cast of insects. Hobbys may be seen hunting for dragonflies and moths.

habilitated into semi-natural social groups. The park has a wide range of Chimpanzees, Woolly Monkeys, Orangutans, Gibbons, Lemurs, Capuchins, Macaques and other monkeys to see. What they think of the humans visitors may be seen in their facial expressions.

**Sculpture by the Lakes** (SY787912) is at Pallington on the north side of the River Frome. The website sums it up, *"Created by renowned sculptor Simon Gudgeon, Sculpture by the Lakes was born from a personal vision of Simon's – to offer enthusiasts an environment which uniquely blends nature's beauty with inspiring art and where visitors can enjoy art without the constriction of enclosed spaces and walls."*

This unique place features large and small pieces, all set in a gentle riverside environment. The effect is spectacular, yet subtle and restful to the visitor. *"Simon Gudgeon has a signature smooth style that wonderfully concentrates spirit and nature. His minimalist, semi-abstract forms depict both movement and emotion of a moment captured with a visual harmony that is unmistakably his own."*

*Sculpture by the Lakes*

### WINFRITH UKAEA

Winfrith (B *wīnn frud*, White Stream) was a United Kingdom Atomic Energy Authority site which opened in 1958. It was involved with the research and development of nuclear reactors. Perhaps the most famous and innovative was Dragon, a high temperature experimental reactor which used helium as coolant. Completed in 1962, it operated until 1976.

Eight other reactors were built here, including a Steam Generating Heavy Water Reactor (SGHWR). This unusual design operated successfully from 1968 to 1990, feeding 100MW into the National Grid. All of the reactors were closed down by 1995 and the site is now being decommissioned. The aim is to fully remediate and restore the area to publicly accessible heathland by 2021.

*Sculpture by the Lakes at Pallington*

Swanage Steam Railway

*1960s British Railways Weymouth poster*    *1930s London & Southwestern Railway poster*

## GETTING TO DORSET

With its central position on the southern coast of England, Dorset is easily accessible by air, road, rail and ferry from the UK, Ireland and Europe.

### AIR TRAVEL

Dorset is served by four regional airports, which together offer services from nearly 200 places across the UK and Europe. The main airlines are easyJet, FlyBe, Ryanair and Thomson, but a host of other operators also offer flights.

**Bristol Airport** (BRS) BS48 3DY is 8mi south of Bristol on the A38
bristolairport.co.uk
Tel 0871 3344444

**Bournemouth Airport** (BOH) BH23 6SE is 4mi northeast of the town off the B3073
bournemouthairport.com
Tel 01202 364000

**Exeter International Airport** (EXT) EX5 2BD is 4mi east of the city off the A30
exeter-airport.co.uk
Tel 01392 367433

**Southampton Airport (SOU)** SO18 2NL is 4mi northeast of the city.
southamptonairport.com
Tel 0844 4817777

### FERRIES

Dorset has now only one operational ro-ro ferry port, at Poole, which runs services to France and the Channel Islands. Brittany Ferries operates from Poole to Cherbourg. Condor Ferries run services from Poole to Jersey and Guernsey, then onward to St Malo.
brittany-ferries.co.uk
condorferries.co.uk

### RAIL TRAVEL

Dorset has excellent rail connections provided by three lines. These run from Waterloo to Weymouth, Weymouth to Exeter via Gillingham and Bristol to Weymouth. All of these lines go through Dorchester.

The First Great Western website is recommended for planning and booking as it does not

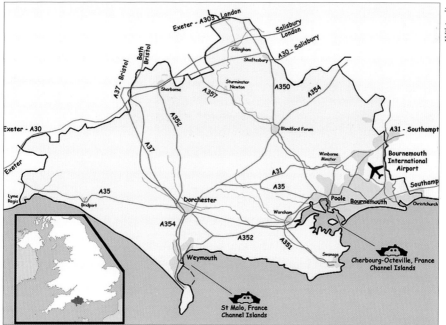

*Wikipedia*

*Map of Dorset showing main transport routes*

surcharge for credit cards, first-greatwestern.co.uk Southwest Trains website, southwest-trains.co.uk and National Rail are also useful for planning nationalrail.co.uk

*Freedom of the Severn-Solent* is an excellent idea for those planning several journeys over a number of days. Passes are valid off peak during the week-end, all day at weekends and on Bank Holidays, railrover.org/pages/freedom-of-severn-and-solent-rover

## ROAD TRAVEL

Although there are no motorways in Dorset, the county has excellent access to the national motorway system from London and the southeast, the north and the southwest.

*easyJet flies to many destinations*

*FlyBe offers a wide range of UK and European destinations*

# Getting Around in Purbeck

*The X53 bus*

Lyme Regis, Charmouth, Bridport, Abbotsbury, Weymouth, Wool and Wareham to Poole. Tickets offer unlimited travel for a day. The service is ideal for walkers planning routes along the South West Coast Path. Full timetables at firstgroup.com/ukbus/dorset

## TRAVEL WITHIN DORSET

### DRIVING

Within Dorset there are sections of dual carriageway and many towns are bypassed. However during busy periods progress may be slow due to most of the roads being narrow and twisting as well as passing through small villages.

Accordingly, driving times between different parts of the county may be relatively long. With such a lot of beautiful scenery and so many places to visit, this should be regarded as a bonus to the visitor.

It is the quietness of the thousands of miles of narrow, single track lanes which wind between hedges across the countryside that are one of Dorset's principal attractions. However, great care needs to be taken as the locals do not drive slowly. Very large tractors, lorries and other traffic are frequently encountered.

### BUSES

Dorset offers two special treats. The Route 50 Purbeck Breezer starts at Bournemouth train station then follows the coastline to Sandbanks. It then takes the chain ferry to Studland before ending up at Swanage. Open top buses are used on the year-round route.

The X53 Jurassic Coast Bus Service operates every two hours in the summer from Exeter via Sidford, Beer, Seaton,

### CYCLING

Dorset offers a great deal to cyclists, however many of the main roads are not recommended. Most are narrow, with many blind summits and bends, and can be very congested at peak periods.

The good news is that the county has thousands of miles of delightful side roads and lanes to explore. Cycling is perhaps the best way to enjoy the Dorset countryside as the slow pace allows far more appreciation of the surroundings.

### WALKING

The county is a paradise for all walkers, ranging from serious long distance types doing the South West Coast Path to those taking a short stroll. Walks are suggested through-

*The many quiet lanes are great for cyclists*

*Dorset has many fingerposts*

*Walking on the Jurassic Coast*

out the book and in the Itineraries Section. A variety of books about walking routes are included in the bibliography.

## TRAVEL INFORMATION

The dorsetforyou.com website has a great deal of useful information about all forms of travel within the county. This includes car, bus, cycling, walking, rail, boat and air. The live travel alerts are especially useful: mapping.dorsetforyou.com/TravelDorset

Another excellent website for Dorset transport and travel information is dorset-transport.info. It offers live transport information on aircraft movements, trains and National Express coaches. Some buses also have tracking devices.

*Dorset county sign*

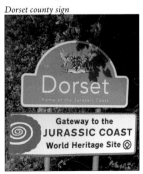

### DISTANCES BY ROAD FROM DORCHESTER

| WITHIN DORSET | | mi | km |
|---|---|---|---|
| Dorchester | Blandford Forum | 18 | 29 |
| | Bournemouth | 29 | 46 |
| | Bridport | 15 | 24 |
| | Christchurch | 34 | 56 |
| | Exmouth | 60 | 97 |
| | Lyme Regis | 26 | 42 |
| | Poole | 24 | 39 |
| | Portland Bill | 17 | 27 |
| | Shaftesbury | 31 | 49 |
| | Sherborne | 20 | 32 |
| | Swanage | 26 | 42 |
| | Wareham | 20 | 33 |
| | Weymouth | 9 | 14 |
| **NEARBY AIRPORTS** | | **mi** | **km** |
| Dorchester | Bournemouth Airport | 29 | 46 |
| | Bristol Airport | 62 | 100 |
| | Exeter Airport | 55 | 89 |
| | Gatwick | 138 | 222 |
| | Heathrow | 111 | 178 |
| | Luton Airport | 144 | 232 |
| | Southampton Airport | 55 | 89 |
| | Stansted | 173 | 278 |
| **FERRY PORTS** | | **mi** | **km** |
| Dorchester | Dover | 199 | 320 |
| | Holyhead | 339 | 546 |
| | Hull | 309 | 497 |
| | Newcastle | 379 | 609 |
| | Pembroke | 213 | 343 |
| | Plymouth | 99 | 159 |
| **UK TOWNS, CITIES AND PLACES** | | **mi** | **km** |
| Dorchester | Aberdeen | 587 | 945 |
| | Birmingham | 169 | 273 |
| | Bristol | 62 | 100 |
| | Edinburgh | 457 | 735 |
| | Exeter | 55 | 89 |
| | Inverness | 612 | 985 |
| | John o'Groats | 728 | 1172 |
| | Lands End | 176 | 283 |
| | London Centre | 130 | 209 |
| | London M25 | 113 | 182 |
| | Salisbury | 40 | 65 |
| | Yeovil | 21 | 34 |

# Purbeck - Places to Visit

## What to See & Do in Purbeck

Purbeck offers the visitor a huge range of things to see and do within a relatively small area. Whatever your interest, whether it be archaeology, history, old churches and castles or nationally important formal gardens, it is here.

**Museums** The county features a large number of museums, from the world class Tank Museum to the tiniest specialist village heritage centre. All are interesting and staffed by enthusiastic people who love to tell the story of their museum.

**The National Trust** maintains a variety of properties here. These include Corfe Castle, Clouds Hill and Studland in Purbeck. Major sites in private hands include Lulworth Cove and Castle as well as many museums and nature reserves.

**Nature** enthusiasts will not be disappointed as the county is a year round destination for bird watchers. It is famous for its wild flowers, butterflies and dragonflies. With the 95mi (155km) long Jurassic Coast UNESCO World Heritage Site and nearly 60 varied nature reserves, there is plenty of scope.

**Walkers** will find Purbeck very welcoming, with its huge network of paths, long distance and shorter. Routes can be planned by combining information in this guide with the relevant Ordnance Survey map. Alternatively there are many walking books available. Tour guides also lead groups in many places.

*Wareham is on the River Frome*

**Cycling** Cyclists will find the thousands of miles of winding hedge-lined lanes very enticing. There is no better way to observe the life of the countryside than on an ambling bike ride. The more energetic cyclist will find a large variety of suggested routes in leaflets at the VICs.

**Activities** For people who prefer more organised activities there is a wide range on offer, particularly in the vicinity of Poole, Bournemouth, Christchurch and Weymouth. These cover everything expected of prime seaside resorts with things to do for every age and inclination.

**Coastline** For many the prime attraction of Dorset is its coastline, with many superb beaches. Those at Poole, Bournemouth, Weymouth and Swanage have traditional seaside facilities and entertainments during the summer. People who prefer quiet coves or extensive beaches will not be disappointed, especially in the winter.

**All-Year Attraction** Dorset is a county which will reward the visitor at any time of year and in any weather. That so many visitors come back time and again is testament to the place, but also to the welcome afforded by the Dorset folk.

**Accommodation** This guide specifically does not cover information about accommodation, eating out or shopping as these are well covered by annual tourist guides and subject to frequent change. Dorset offers everything from five star hotels, self catering and bed & breakfast to campsites.

**Eating Out** ranges from top class restaurants to very good chip shops. Dorset offers an excellent range of local produce including prime beef, lamb, pork and seafood as well as fruit and vegetables in season. Few are disappointed.

**Shopping** The many small towns and villages have retained a wide selection of local shops. These include butchers, bakers, fish shops, drapers, bookshops, hardware stores, newsagents and antique outlets and other interesting businesses.

*Tyneham and Worbarrow Bay from Tyneham Cap*

## Visitor Information Centres
visit-dorset.com

There are several Visitor Information Centres in Dorset, all in the main towns and villages. All can be found on visit-dorset.com This website is the Official Dorset Tourism Information Site and covers the huge range of things to see and do in Dorset.

Brochures may also be requested from this website covering Christchurch & Rural Dorset, West Dorset, Swanage & Purbeck as well as the main Dorset Guide.

**Discover Purbeck Information Centre**, Wareham Library, South Street, Wareham, Purbeck BH20 4LR
dorsetforyou.com/396688 Tel 01929 552740

**Swanage Tourist Information Centre**, The White House, Shore Road, Swanage BH19 1LB Tel 01929 422885

Other information sources include visitor attractions, museums, local shops, accommodation providers and rural post offices. Books and guides are available from VICs, local bookshops and visitor attractions, as well as online.

### Archaeology - Iron Age

Flowers Barrow .....................................

### Archaeology - Saxon

Wareham Town Walls.......................................

## Art & Craft

L'Artishe Gallery & Studio, 71 High Street, Swanage, Dorset BH19 2LY
lartishegallery.com Tel 01929 425050
*"Contemporary purpose built art gallery that exhibits modern art and crafts."*

**Sculpture by the Lakes**, Pallington Lakes, Dorchester DT2 8QU sculpturebythelakes.co.uk Tel 07720 637 808.............................................

### Beaches, Coast & Cliffs

Ballard Down ....................................................
Bindon Hill.......................................................
Brownsea Island ...............................................
Chapman's Pool, rocky bay, cliffs.....................
Dancing Ledge
Durdle Door, shingle beaches, cliffs.................
Durlston Head, cliffs .........................................
Fossil Forest, Lulworth......................................
Gad Cliff ...........................................................
Kimmeridge, rocks, cliffs..................................
Lulworth Cove, sand, rocks, cliffs....................
Old Harry Rocks ..............................................

*Sculpture by the Lakes*

*Corfe Castle*

River Frome, Arne.............................
Shell Beach, Studland........................
Shipstal Point, Arne ........................
St Aldhelm's Head, cliffs ...................
Studland, sandy beach.......................
Swanage, sandy beach, cliffs ..............
Swyre Head ....................................
Tilly Whim Caves.............................
White Nothe, cliffs, rocky beach ...................
Worbarrow Bay, sand, shingle, cliffs................

## BOAT TRIPS

**Brownsea Island Ferries**, Hethfelton, East
Stoke, Wareham, Dorset  BH20 6HJ
brownseaislandferries.com  Tel 01929 462383
Boat trips from Poole Quay and Sandbanks
to Brownsea Island,  also from Poole Quay to
Swanage and Wareham.

**Greenslade Pleasure Boats**, The Orange
Kiosk, Poole Quay, Dorset DT15 1HJ
greensladepleasureboats.co.uk
Tel 01202 669955  Boat trips from Poole Quay
to Brownsea Island, Swanage and Wareham

## CASTLES

*Studland Beach*

**Corfe Castle**, Purbeck BH20 5EZ
nationaltrust.org.uk/corfe-castle
Tel 01929 481 294   One of the most romantic
ruined castles in England ...........................................

**Lulworth Castle**, East Lulworth, Purbeck
BH20 5QS
lulworth.com  Tel 01929 400 352
Partially restored  17th cent. mock castle .........

## CHURCHES

Arne Church ......................................................
Bere Regis Church.............................................
Moreton Church ...............................................
St Aldhelm's Chapel, Isle of Purbeck..............
Steeple Church.................................................
Studland Church ..............................................
Wareham,  St Martins........................................
Worth Matravers Church ................................

## EVENTS & FESTIVALS

**Dorset Art Weeks** dorsetartweeks.co.uk
Annually in late May and early June

**Dorset Food Week**
visit-dorset.com  late October/early November

**The Purbeck Film Festival**  purbeckfilm.com
 Tel 07443 468850  Held in October

## MUSEUMS - MILITARY

**The Tank Museum**, Linsay Rd, Bovington,
Purbeck  BH20 6JG
tankmuseum.org  Tel 01929 405 096
Hugely impressive collection of tanks .............

## MUSEUMS - MAIN

**Dorset County Museum**, High West Street,
Dorchester DT1 1XA
dorsetcountymuseum.org  Tel 01305 262735
Excellent and essential visit..............................

**Poole Museum**, 4 High Street, Poole
BH15 1BW  boroughofpoole.com/museums
Tel  01202 262 600
Very good and interesting museum ................

### MUSEUMS - SMALL & SPECIALIST

**Langton Matravers Museum**, St George's Close, Langton Matravers BH19 3HZ
langtonia.org.uk ...............................................

**Swanage Museum & Heritage Centre**, The Square, Swanage BH19 2LJ swanagemuseum. co.uk Tel 01929 475836 ................................

**Wareham Town Museum**, 3 East Street, Wareham BH20 4NN warehammuseum.co.uk Tel 01929 553448............................................

### MUSEUMS - OUTSIDE DORSET

**Ashmolean Museum**, Beaumont Street, Oxford OX1 2PH
ashmolean.org Tel 01865 278000
Many artefacts from Dorset excavations

**Exeter Museum** (Royal Albert Memorial Museum), Queen Street, Exeter EX4 3RX
rammuseum.org.uk Tel 01392 265858
Many artefacts from Dorset excavations

**Natural History Museum**, Cromwell Road, London SW7 5BD nhm.ac.uk
Tel 020 7942 5000 Many fossils from Dorset including large Pleisiosaurs and Ichthyosaurs

**Salisbury Museum**, The Kings House, 65 The Close, Salisbury SP1 2EN
salisburymuseum.org.uk Tel 01722 332151
Many artefacts from Dorset excavations

**Wiltshire Museum**, 41 Long Street, Devizes, Wiltshire SN10 1NS
wiltshire museum.org.uk Tel 01380 727369
Many artefacts from Dorset excavations

### NATURE

**Arne RSPB Reserve**, east of Wareham, Purbeck BH20 5BJ rspb.org.uk
Tel 01929 553360 Wonderful heathland reserve overlooking Poole Harbour ................

**Brownsea Island**, Poole Harbour BH13 7EE
nationaltrust.org.uk/brownsea-island
Tel 01202 707 744
Essential destination for all birders.................

*Avocets can be seen at Arne and on Brownsea Island*

**Durlston Country Park**, Lighthouse Road, Swanage BH19 2JL durlston.co.uk
Tel 01929 424443 This National Nature Reserve is one of the best places for wildlife in Dorset and is an essential visit..........................

**Dorset Wildlife Trust**, Brooklands Farm, Forston, Dorchester DT2 7AA
dorsetwildlifetrust.org.uk Tel 01305 264620

### NATURE - JURASSIC COAST

**The Jurassic Coast, Dorset and East Devon World Heritage Site** jurassiccoast.org Runs for 95mi (155km) from Orcombe Point near Exmouth to Old Harry Rocks in Purbeck.........

**Jurassica** *"will be the world's most spectacular attraction celebrating the lost world of Prehistoric Earth. There will be an aquarium, featuring animatronic Jurassic marine reptiles, the sea monsters of prehistoric Earth. There will be three galleries featuring fossil collections from the Natural History Museum and world-class specimens currently in the hands of private collectors."* jurassica.org

*Fossil ammonites*

*The Tank Museum*

**Kimmeridge Fossil Museum**, Kimmeridge, Purbeck BH20 5PE theetchescollection.org is due to open in 2016.  It will house over 2,000 fossils collected locally by Steve Etches
**Purbeck Marine Wildlife Reserve,**
Kimmeridge Bay, Purbeck BH20 5PF
dorsetwildlifetrust.org.uk Tel 01929 481044
Unique marine reserve.....................................

**Studland Visitor Centre**, Knoll Beach, Studland, Purbeck BH19 3AQ nationaltrust.
org.uk/studland-beach Tel 01929 450500 Information on the local habitats and wildlife in the area and on the Jurassic Coast

### Visitor Attractions

**Cloud's Hill**, Bovington, Purbeck BH20 7NQ
nationaltrust.org.uk/clouds-hill
Tel 01929 405 616.............................................

**Corfe Castle**, Purbeck BH20 5EZ
nationaltrust.org.uk/corfe-castle
Tel 01929 481 294   One of the most romantic ruined castles in England .........................................

*Corfe Castle from the station*

**Lulworth Castle**, East Lulworth, Purbeck BH20 5QS
lulworth.com  Tel 01929 400 352
Partially restored  17th cent. mock castle .........

**Lulworth Cove Heritage Centre**, Main Road, West Lulworth, Dorset BH20 5RQ
lulworth.com/jurassic-coast  Tel 01929 400587 Geological displays, visitor information, shop and toilets; do not miss the excellent Jurassic Jaws exhibition upstairs (entry fee).

**Monkey World**, Longthorns, Wareham BH20 6HH Off the A352, north of Wool
monkeyworld.org  Tel 01929 462537  Many species of rescued apes and monkeys..............

**Swanage Railway**, Station House, Swanage BH19 1HB
swanagerailway.co.uk  Tel 01929 425800 Steam trains Swanage to Corfe Castle .................

**The Blue Pool and Wareham Bears**, south of Wareham BH20 5AR off the A351
bluepooluk.com  Tel 01929 551408
Old china clay pit ...............................................

**The Tank Museum**, Linsay Rd, Bovington, Purbeck  BH20 6JG
tankmuseum.org  Tel 01929 405 096
Hugely impressive collection of tanks .............

**Tyneham**, Lulworth Ranges, Purbeck, Dorset BH20 5QF tynehamopc.org
Tel 01929 404912; Lulworth Range Control Tel 01929 404819
Village evacuated in 1943 and remains part of the MOD Lulworth Ranges.  Open most week-ends, on holidays and for all of August.

*Silver-studded Blue butterfly at Higher Hyde Heath*

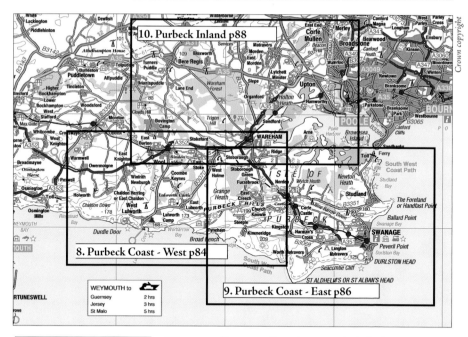

*Crown copyright*

10. Purbeck Inland p88

8. Purbeck Coast - West p84

9. Purbeck Coast - East p86

WEYMOUTH to
Guernsey — 2 hrs
Jersey — 3 hrs
St Malo — 5 hrs

## COUNTRYSIDE CODE

*Please observe these guidelines:*

1. Always use stiles and gates, and close gates behind you.
2. Always ask permission before entering farmland.
3. Keep to paths and avoid fields of grass and crops.
4. Do not disturb livestock.
5. Take your litter away with you and do not light fires.
6. Do not pollute water courses.
7. Never disturb nesting birds.
8. Do not pick wild flowers or dig up plants.
9. Drive and park with care and attention, do not obstruct or endanger others, park responsibly.
10. Take care near cliffs and beaches, particularly with children and pets. Some beaches are dangerous.
11. Walkers should take adequate clothes, wear suitable footwear and tell someone of their plans.
12. Above all, please respect the life of the countryside - leave only footprints, take only photographs and pleasant memories.

*Notice: Most of the sites in this guide are open to the public and have marked access; many are on private land. No right of access is implied; if in doubt it is always polite to ask. Many roads and tracks are rights of way, but not all are.*

**What to Do and See** A selection of suggested itineraries is included in the following pages. These cover all of the main sites of interest in Purbeck. Each excursion is designed to take a day, with plenty of time for getting there, exploration and a picnic or meal along the way. Many of the places covered in the Introduction and Gazetteer are listed in each section with page numbers for reference.

**Private Transport** The itineraries here all assume the use of a car to reach the places mentioned during the course of a day, or longer. Many could also be done by bicycle or by a combination of public transport and walking, though this would take longer.

**Public Transport** The dorsetforyou.com website has a great deal of information about all forms of travel within the county, including by car, bus, cycling, walking, rail, boat and air. The live travel alerts are especially useful: mapping.dorsetforyou.com/TravelDorset

Another excellent website for Dorset transport and travel information is dorset-transport.info. It offers real-time transport information on aircraft movements, trains and National Express coaches. Some buses also have tracking devices.

**Access to the Outdoors** is normally free and available at all times at the sites mentioned. Most of the museums, heritage centres and other visitor attractions charge for entry. Some, very helpfully, include multiple visits for a year. Many have seasonal opening, but may be visited by arrangement at other times, or have special openings. Contact should be made well in advance since, out of season, many sites are unstaffed.

**Car Parking** is charged for throughout Dorset, even at seemingly remote sites. Membership of the National Trust and the RSPB is strongly recommended. Car parking permits are available, but there is no comprehensive scheme for the whole county, making them of little use to visitors. It is strongly recommended to have a good supply of £1 coins on hand at all times.

**Walking** Purbeck is a walker's paradise, with thousands of miles of quiet country lanes, byways, tracks, ridgeways and footpaths. This guide does not suggest detailed walking routes as exploring is half of the delight of any visit. For those wishing such directions there is a good selection of walks books available. Visitor information centres, nature reserves and most attractions stock leaflets giving current details of opening times, prices, walks, etc.

**Country Lanes** Purbeck has thousands of miles of highly attractive country lanes. These are usually narrow, winding, and have few passing places. Locals tend to drive quite fast, while traffic may include huge tractors, cattle, sheep, cyclists and pedestrians. All road

---

### WHAT TO DO AND SEE - SOME SUGGESTED ITINERARIES AND WALKS
#### 45 SITES TO VISIT - INSIDE BACK COVER

##### ISLE OF PURBECK ITINERARIES

| | | |
|---|---|---|
| 8. | White Nothe to Tyneham | 84 |
| 9. | Kimmeridge to Studland | 86 |
| 10. | Wareham, Bovington & Bere Regis | 88 |

##### SOME COASTAL WALKING DISTANCES

| | mi | km |
|---|---|---|
| White Nothe to Durdle Door | 3.4 | 5.4 |
| Durdle Door to Lulworth Cove | 1.2 | 1.9 |
| Lulworth Cove to Tyneham | 4.4 | 7.1 |
| Tyneham to Kimmeridge Bay | 2.8 | 4.4 |
| Kimmeridge Bay to St Aldhelm's Head | 6.0 | 9.6 |
| St Aldhelm's Head to Durlston Head | 5.5 | 8.9 |
| Durlston Head to Swanage Pier | 2.1 | 3.3 |
| Swanage Pier to Old Harry Rocks | 3.3 | 5.3 |
| Old Harry Rocks to South Haven Point | 1.5 | 2.4 |
| White Nothe to South Haven Point | 30.1 | 48.3 |

##### SOME INLAND WALKING DISTANCES

| | mi | km |
|---|---|---|
| Priests' Way Swanage to Worth Matravers | 3 | 4.9 |
| Wareham Two Rivers - Frome & Piddle | 3 | 4.9 |
| Ballard Down & Studland Circular | 4.5 | 7.2 |
| Corfe Castle to Kingston circular | 5.5 | 8.9 |
| Lawrence of Arabia Way; Bovington to Moreton | 6.8 | 10.9 |
| Purbeck Way; Wareham to Chapman's Pool | 28 | 45.1 |
| Purbeck Way West; Wareham to Coombe Keynes | 16 | 25.8 |

---

users should proceed with care and attention, no matter how rural and quiet the road might appear.

Although not specifically mentioned in the itineraries, the verges, hedges and field boundaries throughout Dorset are a haven for wildlife, including wildflowers, birds, butterflies and mammals. Visitors are advised to slow down, keep their eyes and ears on the alert and to enjoy the deep peace of the Purbeck countryside.

**Maps** The use of OS Explorer 1:25,000 or OS Landranger 1:25,000 maps, or their digital equivalent, is assumed. The 1:25,000 scale maps are by far the best for exploration as they provide excellent detail. The 1:250,000 maps used throughout this book are intended only for orientation, and are of too small a scale for walking or cycling. Each itinerary lists the OS maps for that particular area.

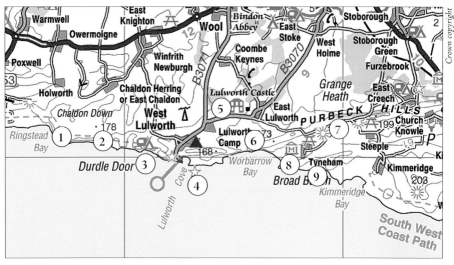

*Crown copyright*

## PURBECK COAST - WEST
## THE WHITE NOTHE TO TYNEHAM

**THE DISTRICT OF PURBECK** is bounded to the south by a dramatic chalk ridge from the White Nothe to Old Harry Rocks, broken by bays and valleys in places. The whole western coastline described here is criss-crossed by lanes, track and footpaths. These allow free access all the way from Ringstead Bay to Lulworth Cove.

**Cliffs** From the White Nothe to Worbarrow Bay, high chalk cliffs dominate the coast, reaching 175m at the latter. Harder limestone appears at Durdle Door, Lulworth Cove and the Gad Cliffs. Off-lying limestone ledges also occur in many places at the bottom of the cliffs.

**Lulworth Army Ranges** From Lulworth Cove to Kimmeridge Bay the whole area forms part of Lulworth Ranges. Access is only allowed here when the ranges are closed. This means most weekends and holidays as well as all of August. The upside is that this large area of coastline and heathland has remained undeveloped for 70 years, preserving its wildlife.

**The Purbeck Hills** From Worbarrow Bay eastwards the chalk ridge forms the Purbeck Hills, the backbone of the "Isle". Tyneham is at the westward end of a fertile clay valley that goes all the way to Swanage in the east.

West Purbeck has a great deal to offer the walker with everything from a section of the South West Coast Path, to gentle strolls. The chalk coastal ridge is undulating due to "bottoms" such as Scratchy Bottom, Lulworth Cove or Arish Mell.

This means that what looks like an easy stroll is in fact quite a strenuous walk. As a result, places like Lulworth Cove and Durdle Door can be crowded, while a few hundreds metres away it may be very quiet.

**ORDNANCE SURVEY 1:50,000 & 1:25,000 MAPS**

OS Landranger Map 194 Dorchester & Weymouth; Map 195 Bournemouth & Purbeck
OS Explorer Map OL15 Purbeck & South Dorset

## PURBECK COAST - WEST
### THE WHITE NOTHE TO TYNEHAM

**1. The White Nothe** (page 26) is the most westerly point of the Purbeck cliffs. This imposing chalk 169m headland offers stunning views over Weymouth Bay and along the coast to the east.
**Burning, or Holworth, Cliff** is a large area of undercliffs formed by regular landslides. The beach walk from Ringstead Bay to the foot of the White Nothe, can only be done on a falling tide.
**Smuggler's Path** is a short but very steep 300m climb from the bottom of the cliff.

**2. Swyre Head** (98m, page 26) is about 1,200m west of Durdle Door and offers fine views in both directions along this spectacular coastline.

**3. Durdle Door** (page 26) is one of Dorset's iconic natural features, very much photographed, and yet never fails to impress. Perhaps best visited when the evening sun is low, the shingle beaches can be followed for about 1,000m in each direction. Durdle Door can be reached from the Newland Farm carpark or from Lulworth Cove.

**4. Lulworth Cove** (page 26) is one of the most visited coastal features in Britain. This almost perfectly round, shallow bay has a gently sloping sand and shingle beach. There are fine panoramic views from the cliffs on both sides of the cove. The headland on the west side has amazing contortions on the seaward side, similar to those at the nearby Crumple.
**Stair Hole and the Crumple** (page 26), about 250m from the carpark, has a large natural arch where the sea has broken through. The limestone here has undergone violent earth movements.
**West Lulworth Heritage Centre** (page 27) tells the story of Lulworth, with displays on geology, fossils, landscape and local history. There is also a gift shop; it is open all year and has a large car park.
**Lulworth Walks** can be long or short, depending on time and fitness as there is a huge number of paths and tracks which can be followed.

**5. Lulworth Castle** (page 27) is a partially restored 17th century mock castle built as a hunting lodge. It is surrounded by mature woodland and open spaces.

**6. Lulworth Ranges** (page 28) are part of the Armoured Fighting Vehicles Gunnery School at Lulworth Camp. They are closed when in operation; red flags are flown and the gates are locked. The Ranges are open at weekends, on holidays and during August.
*All of the following places are within the Ranges:*
**The Fossil Forest** (page 28) is on the coast about 400m east of Lulworth Cove. Fossilised tree trunks are surrounded by ancient stromatolites.
**Bindon Hill** (168m, page 28) is a good place to look for Lulworth Skipper butterflies. There are splendid views over the cliffs and bays to the east.
**Mupe Bay** (page 28) may be only 2.5mi (4km) along the coast from Durdle Door, but it feels like a world away. Even in high summer there are never many people here. From the top of the cliff there are wonderful views across to Worbarrow Bay and beyond, with Mupe Ledges and Rocks in the foreground. The beach is accessible by a steep path. Though only 2mi (3km) from Lulworth Cove the path is very steep in places, making it seem further.
**Arish Mell** (page 28), about 1,000m to the east, is inaccessible due to contamination, and must be admired from the coastal path.

**7. Povington Hill** (187m, page 30) is the highest point on the road that follows the Purbeck Hills ridge eastwards from Lulworth. There are panoramic views to the south from this and other points.

**8. Tyneham** (page 30), or *"the village that time forgot"*, is reached from the ridge road. This isolated valley, along with its coastline, has a special charm. The village has a feeling of sadness about it.
**Worbarrow Bay** (page 29) has 1,300m curve of sand and shingle, backed by dramatic chalk cliffs. There is a fine viewpoint at Worbarrow Tout.
**Flowers Barrow** (page 28) is a large Iron Age hillfort perched 170m above the north side of Worbarrow Bay. It is slowly being lost to the sea as the cliffs are constantly being eroded.

**9. Gad Cliff** (page 30) reaches 130m below Tyneham Cap page 208). This dramatic 2mi (3km) rock face looks smooth from the west and like jagged teeth from the east.
**Brandy Bay** (page 30), below Tyneham Cap has many offlying rocks, including Long Ebb and Broad Bench, over which rough seas break spectacularly.

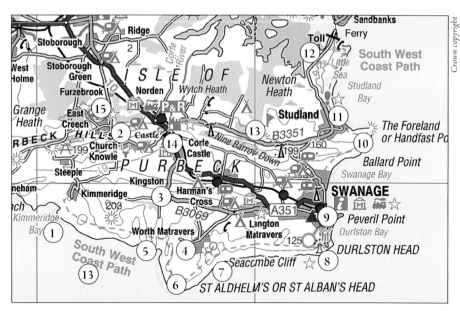

*Crown copyright*

## PURBECK COAST - EAST
## KIMMERIDGE TO STUDLAND

THE ISLE OF PURBECK is smaller than the modern administrative district. It extends north from Flowers Barrow to the River Frome and thence to Wareham and Poole Harbour. This area is bounded to the south by great limestone cliffs and to the north by low-lying heathland. The spine of the Purbeck Hills runs across the centre, separated from the coastal ridge by a fertile valley.

**Corfe Castle** is an essential visit, with its fairytale castle, ancient limestone houses, steam trains and dramatic situation. The best views are from West Hill at dawn or East Hill at sunset, especially when mist shrouds the countryside, or from Kingston to the south.

**Inland Villages** include Church Knowle, Steeple, Kimmeridge, Worth Matravers and Langton Matravers. These ancient, small settlements all have their own charm and interesting history.

**Durlston Country Park** is one of the best nature reserves in Dorset with over 500 species of wild flowers, 33 of butterflies and 270 of birds. Not far behind are Ballard Down and Studland Heath. The Purbeck Hills are also good for butterflies and wild flowers.

**Seaside Resorts** Purbeck has two popular seaside resorts, which could hardly be more different. Swanage is a slightly genteel, smaller version of Weymouth and much less commercial. It has a beautiful, sheltered situation with a fine long sandy beach. Studland has a beautiful 4mi (6km) beach and is almost totally non-commercialised because it belongs to the National Trust.

**The South West Coast Path** includes essential visits such as Kimmeridge Bay, Chapman's Pool, St Aldhelm's Head and Durlston Head. Throughout the whole area there is a maze of quiet country lanes, tracks and footpaths. Some are signposted or waymarked, but many are not. In this busy area of Dorset it is easy to get away from the crowds in unspoilt countryside. Conversely, there is also plenty on offer for those preferring busy towns.

---

**ORDNANCE SURVEY 1:50,000 & 1:25,000 MAPS**
OS Landranger Map 195 Bournemouth & Purbeck
OS Explorer Map OL15 Purbeck & South Dorset

---

## Purbeck Coast - East
## Kimmeridge to Studland

**1. Kimmeridge Bay** (page 32) is ringed by low cliffs with bands of clay, shale and cementstone. The Flats and Ledges, visible only at low tide, are of hard limestone, ideal for rock pooling or fossil hunting. Kimmeridge is about 5mi (8km) southwest of Corfe Castle. The Jurassic Kimmeridge Clay Formation is famous for its abundant fossils. **Gad Cliff** (130m) to the west, looks like a giant limestone saw blade from the hill above the bay. The "Nodding Donkey" at the west end of the bay extracts oil from Jurassic strata 350m underground. **Purbeck Marine Wildlife Reserve** extends from Mupe Bay to St Aldhelm's Head. The Marine Centre has aquaria and helpful marine wardens. **Clavell Tower**, a 19th century folly, is now available as an esoteric holiday let.

**2. Church Knowle** (page 49) is a pretty little village which snuggles below the Purbeck Hills. It has a fine Norman church and a traditional pub. **Steeple** (page 49), 2mi (3km) further west, is famous for its connection to the US flag. The design is based on the Lawrence coat of arms, which can be seen in the Norman church.

**3. Kingston** (130m, page 48) on a ridge 1.5mi (2.5km) south of Corfe Castle has pretty cottages and panoramic views. Its main claim to fame is the excellent and very popular Scotts Arms pub.

**4. Worth Matravers** (page 35, 48), the most southerly and picturesque of these villages, is about 1.5mi (2.5km) southeast of Kingston. Benjamin Jesty, who discovered a cure for smallpox, and his wife, are buried in the graveyard here. The unique local pub, the Square and Compass should not be missed.

**5. Chapman's Pool** (page 34) is about 1,000m down a steep footpath from a carpark at Renscombe Farm. This delightful bay is never busy and the shoreline is an excellent place for fossil hunting.

**6. St Aldhelm's Head** (108m, page 34) is the most southerly point on Purbeck, with superb views. The unusually-built chapel may be Norman. There was an important radar station here in WWII.

**7. Winspit** (page 35) is a small bay east of St Aldhelm's Head. The cliffs are pock-marked with old limestone quarries, now home to many bats.

**8. Durlston Country Park** (113ha, page 38) is one of the prime destinations in Dorset for anyone interested in nature. The Visitor Centre has interactive displays, a gallery, shop and restaurant. Waymarked paths, information on daily sightings and events are all available there and online. The reserve is deservedly famous for its diversity of species of wild flowers, butterflies and birds. Many come to seek the rare Early-spider Orchids or Lulworth Skipper butterflies.

**Anvil Point Lighthouse** (page 39) is a waypoint for shipping between Portland Bill and the Solent. **Tilly Whim Caves** (page 39), next to Anvil Point are former limestone quarries. Many bats roost here so they are not open to the public.

**9. Swanage** (page 40) is a rather elegant and unspoilt seaside resort. Earlier prosperity was based on quarrying of Purbeck Marble and Limestone, especially from the 17th century onwards. **Swanage Steam Railway** (page 41, 47) was formed as a result of the branch line being closed in 1972. Trains now run regularly to Corfe Castle and Norden, as well as occasionally to Wareham.

**10. Ballard Down** (page 42) marks the eastern end of the Jurassic Coast World Heritage Site. This chalk escarpment ends at Handfast Point. **Old Harry Rocks** (page 42) are chalk stacks which extend eastwards from Handfast Point.

**11. Studland Bay** (page 43) has 4mi (6km) of beautiful sands, backed by extensive dunes and the Studland Heath Nature Reserve. The village has a fine Norman church and an excellent pub.

**12. South Haven Point** (page 43) is the terminal for the chain ferry to Sandbanks.

**13. Kingswood Down** (page 42), below Nine Barrow Down, has a panoramic view over Studland.

**14. Corfe Castle** (page 46), a small stone-built village in the centre of Purbeck, is dominated by its romantic and iconic castle, one of the most impressive in England. The National Trust keep the castle, shop, tearoom and visitor centre open all year.

**15. The Blue Pool** (page 47) is an old clay pit at Furzebrook, northwest of Corfe Castle. It has a shop, tearoom, museum and plant centre.

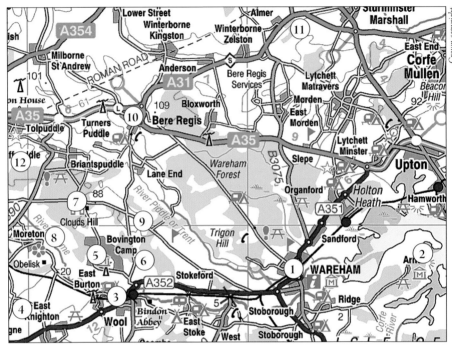

*Crown copyright*

**Northern Purbeck** stretches from Wareham in the east to Bovington in the west and Bere Regis in the north. The Rivers Stour and Piddle traverse the mostly flat landscape, which still retains many areas of heathland. This small, rural region holds some world class places to visit, cultural and natural.

**Wareham** was founded by the Saxons in the 8th century. Its development has always been constrained by its old walls and the surrounding terrain. As a result it retains its old character more than any other Dorset town. St Martin's is the only intact Saxon church in the county.

**The Tank Museum** is a world-class collection of military hardware, with an unrivalled display of armoured vehicles, many in working condition. These range from the earliest prototypes to WWI, WWII and modern tanks.

**TE Lawrence**, aka *"Lawrence of Arabia"*, was based at Bovington Camp and lived in the little house at Clouds Hill during this time. He is buried at nearby Moreton and has an effigy in St Martin's Church, Wareham. Aficionados can follow the "Lawrence of Arabia Trail" through Moreton plantation.

**Arne RSPB Reserve**, east of Wareham, is one of the star attractions of Dorset. Over 220 species of birds, 33 of butterflies, 23 of dragonflies, 31 of mammals, all 6 British reptiles and c.500 of wild flowers have been recorded here. This large and varied reserve is a year-round destination.

**Upper Hyde Heath**, near Bovington Camp, is an internationally important nature reserve famous for its butterflies and dragonflies. All six species of British reptiles are present, as well as an interesting selection of plants and birds.

**ORDNANCE SURVEY 1:50,000 & 1:25,000 MAPS**

OS Landranger Map 194 Dorchester & Weymouth; Map 195 Bournemouth & Purbeck
OS Explorer Map OL15 Purbeck & South Dorset

## PURBECK - INLAND
## WAREHAM TO BOVINGTON & BERE REGIS

**1. Wareham** (page 52) stands on a small promontory between the rivers Frome and Piddle, protected by their marshy flood plains. The town retains its Saxon street plan within the Town Walls.

**St Martin's Church** (page 52) is the most complete Saxon church in Dorset and dates from the 11th century. The interior has many ancient wall paintings as well as an effigy of TE Lawrence.

**The Saxon Town Walls** (page 52) surround Wareham on all sides except for the south, which was protected by the river. Still over 4m high, they can be followed for about 1,500m.

**Wareham Quay** (page 53) on the River Frome is highly attractive and unspoilt, with an open square, wooden piles and old stonework. There is access to Poole Harbour via Wareham Channel for shallow-draughted small craft.

**2. Arne RSPB Reserve** (563ha, page 54) is quite simply one of the best nature reserves in the country. It is about 4mi (6km) southeast of Wareham, off the B3075. Its diverse habitats make it an essential visit for wildlife enthusiasts all year round. There is a Visitor Centre, several trails as well as hides overlooking Arne Bay and Middlebere Lake. Nearby, Hartland Moor and Stoborough Heath National Nature Reserves should also be visited.

**3. Wool** (page 66) has a very picturesque old bridge across the River Frome, with an Elizabethan manor behind. The bridge is now bypassed; it is said to be haunted by a coach and horses.

**4. Winfrith and Tadnoll Heaths** (pages 66), south of Moreton are a mixture of dry and wet heathland. The Tadnoll Brook runs through the reserve, which provides habitats for many dragonflies. Silver-studded Blue butterflies are found on the dry heath which also attracts many birds.

**5. The Tank Museum** (page 62) at Bovington Camp is a world class collection covering the development and history of armoured vehicles from the first prototype tank of 1915. The museum has nearly 300 tanks from all over the world as well as about 100 other military vehicles. Many events, including tank action days are held annually.

**6. Monkey World Centre** (page 66) is on Tout Hill about 1mi (1.5km) north of Wool, opposite Bovington Camp. Founded in 1987 by Jim Cronin, the Centre is home to large numbers of rescued and rehabilitated apes and monkeys.

**7. TE Lawrence** lived at Clouds Hill (page 64) from 1923 to 1935, whilst he served in the Army at Bovington Camp. Today the house belongs to the National Trust, who maintain it as it was in 1935.

**8. Moreton** (page 234) is about 3mi (5km) southwest of Clouds Hill. TE Lawrence is buried in the cemetery here. St Nicholas Church in the village has a unique collection of engraved windows by the artist Laurence Whistler.

**9. Higher Hyde Heath** (54ha, page 67) is northeast of Bovington Camp about 1.5mi (2km) east of Clouds Hill. With a wide range of habitats in a relatively small area this is one of the best nature reserves in Dorset. It is famous for its reptiles, butterflies and dragonflies. The best time to visit is late spring and throughout the summer.

**10. Bere Regis** (page 60) is best known for the St John the Baptist Church interior with its very ornate 15th century wooden roof. This was paid for by John Morton, Lord Chancellor to Henry VI.

**Shitterton** (page 61) is a pretty little village with many old thatched cottages. The Bere River protected it from several disastrous fires suffered by its neighbour. Its slightly unfortunate name makes it a favourite for scatological visitors, who will find its signpost hard to remove.

**11. Charborough House** (page 61) is in the extreme northeast of Purbeck. The A31 main road passes around the grounds in a large loop, following the diverted route of a 19th century turnpike. It was here that a meeting was held in 1686 which set the Glorious Revolution of 1688 in motion. The gardens are open to the public on various dates in May.

**12. Sculpture by the Lakes** (page 67) at Pallington is on the north bank of the River Frome about 1.5mi (2.5km) northeast of Moreton. Many pieces by Simon Gudgeon are beautifully placed around old gravel pits amid trees.

Anvil Point Lighthouse, Durlston Country Park

# DORSET BIBLIOGRAPHY

*Durdle Door is probably the most photographed place in Dorset, but never fails to impress.*

## DORSET - GENERAL BOOKS

| | | | |
|---|---|---|---|
| Highways and Byways of Dorset | Sir Frederich Treves | Macmillan | 1906 |
| Purbeck, a brief guide | Robert Westwood | Inspiring Places | 2009 |
| Slow Dorset | Alexandra Richards | Bradt | 2012 |
| Dorset, The Complete Guide | Jo Draper | Dovecote Press | 2003 |
| Dorset, Hampshire & the Isle of Wight | Hancock & Tomlin | Rough Guides | 2013 |
| Dorset Up Along and Down Along | ed MR Dacombe | Women's Institutes | 1951 |
| Dorset | Oeta Whaley | Venton | 2002 |
| Dorset's World Heritage Coast | John Beavis | Tempus | 2004 |

## WALKING

| | | | |
|---|---|---|---|
| 50 Walks in Dorset | AF Stonehouse | AA Publishing | 2013 |
| Dorset Walks | Coduit, Brooks & Viccars | Jarrold | 2006 |
| A Boot Up Dorset's Jurassic Coast | Rodney Legg | PiZX Books | 2008 |
| A Boot Up Purbeck | Rodney Legg | PiZX Books | 2009 |
| South West Coast Path, Exmouth to Poole | Roland Tarr | Aurum Press | 2011 |

## ARCHAEOLOGY

| | | | |
|---|---|---|---|
| Dorset's Archaeology | Peter Stanier | Dorset Books | 2004 |

## HISTORY - GENERAL

| | | | |
|---|---|---|---|
| A History of Dorset | CE Cullingford | Phillimore | 1999 |
| Early Norman Castles Built in Dorset | Ray Baxter | Dorset Castles Research | 2010 |
| Dorset's Best Churches | B Lehane & D Bailey | Dovecote | 2006 |
| Saxons & Vikings | David A Hinton | Dovecote Press | 1998 |
| Dorset in the Age of Steam | Peter Stanier | Dorset Books | 2002 |
| Shipwreck Guide, Dorset & S Devon | Nigel Clarke | Nigel Clarke | |
| Tyneham, A Lost Heritage | Lilian Bond | Dovecote Press | 1984 |

## PLACENAMES AND LANGUAGE

| | | | |
|---|---|---|---|
| The Place-Names of Dorset | Anton Fagersten | Uppsala | 1933 |
| Dorset Place-Names | AD Mills | Countryside Books | 1998 |
| Dorset Place Names | Anthony Poulton-Smith | Amberley | 2010 |

## GEOLOGY AND FOSSILS

| | | | |
|---|---|---|---|
| Fossils & Rocks of the Jurassic Coast | Robert Westwood | Inspiring Places | 2008 |
| Geology of the Jurassic Coast, Purbeck - Weymouth to Studland | P Ensom & M Turnbull | Coastal Publishing | 2011 |
| Wildlife of the Jurassic Coast | Bryan Edwards | Coastal Publishing | 2008 |
| Discover Dorset, Geology | Paul Ensom | Dovecote Press | 1998 |
| Geology of the Dorset Coast | John CW Cope | Geologist's Association | 2012 |

## NATURAL HISTORY - GENERAL

| | | | |
|---|---|---|---|
| Natural History of Dorset | Dorset Wildlife Trust | Dovecote Press | 1997 |
| Dorset, A Naturalist's County | Nigel Webb & Tony Bates | Dovecote Press | 2011 |

## NATURAL HISTORY - BIRDS

| | | | |
|---|---|---|---|
| Collins Bird Guide | Mullarney et al | HarperCollins | 2000 |
| Best Birdwatching Sites in Dorset | Neil Gartshore | Buckingham Press | 2011 |
| Where to Watch Birds in Dorset, Hampshire and IOW | G Green & M Cade | Helm | 2010 |

## NATURAL HISTORY - MARINE

| | | | |
|---|---|---|---|
| Guide to Sea & Shore Life | Gibson, Hextall & Rogers | Oxford | 2001 |

## NATURAL HISTORY - INSECTS

| | | | |
|---|---|---|---|
| Britain's Butterflies | Newland, Still et al | WILDGuides | 2010 |
| Butterflies & Moths | Sterry & Mackay | Dorling Kindersley | 2004 |
| Dragonflies and Damselflies | Brooks and Lewington | British Wildlife Publishing | 2004 |
| Britain's Dragonflies | D Smallshire & A Swash | WILDGuides | 2014 |

## NATURAL HISTORY - FLORA

| | | | |
|---|---|---|---|
| Wild Flowers of Britain & Ireland | Blamey, Fitter & Fitter | A&C Black | 2003 |
| Orchids of Britain & Ireland | Anne & Simon Harrap | A&C Black | 2005 |
| Discovering Dorset's Wild Flowers | Peter Cramb | P&M Cramb | 2013 |
| Wild Flowers of the Dorset Coast Path | Cramb & Cramb | P&M Cramb | 2003 |
| Wild Flower Walks in Dorset | Cramb & Cramb | P&M Cramb | 2006 |
| Shorter Wild Flower Walks in Dorset | Cramb & Cramb | P&M Cramb | 2009 |

## MAPS

| | | | | |
|---|---|---|---|---|
| OS Landranger | Map 194 | Dorchester & Weymouth | Ordnance Survey | 2008 |
| OS Landranger | Map 195 | Bournemouth & Purbeck | Ordnance Survey | 2009 |
| OS Explorer | Map OL15 | Purbeck & South Dorset | Ordnance Survey | 2010 |
| OS Explorer | Map 117 | Cerne Abbas & Bere Regis | Ordnance Survey | 2010 |

# INDEX

*Wareham is on the north bank of the River Frome*

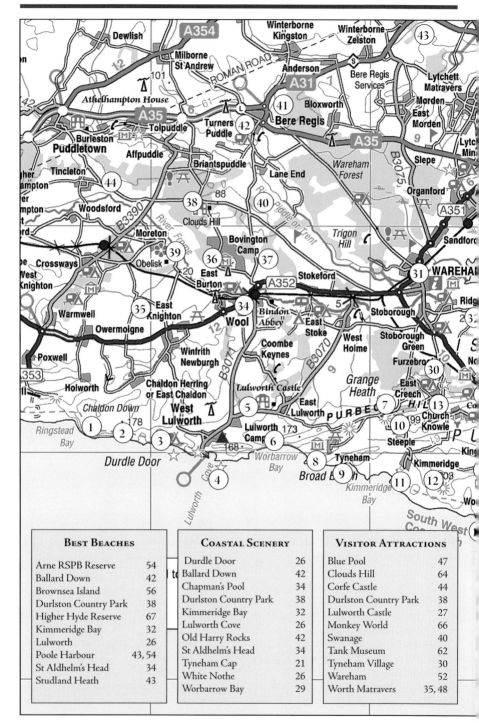

| BEST BEACHES | | COASTAL SCENERY | | VISITOR ATTRACTIONS | |
|---|---|---|---|---|---|
| Arne RSPB Reserve | 54 | Durdle Door | 26 | Blue Pool | 47 |
| Ballard Down | 42 | Ballard Down | 42 | Clouds Hill | 64 |
| Brownsea Island | 56 | Chapman's Pool | 34 | Corfe Castle | 44 |
| Durlston Country Park | 38 | Durlston Country Park | 38 | Durlston Country Park | 38 |
| Higher Hyde Reserve | 67 | Kimmeridge Bay | 32 | Lulworth Castle | 27 |
| Kimmeridge Bay | 32 | Lulworth Cove | 26 | Monkey World | 66 |
| Lulworth | 26 | Old Harry Rocks | 42 | Swanage | 40 |
| Poole Harbour | 43, 54 | St Aldhelm's Head | 34 | Tank Museum | 62 |
| St Aldhelm's Head | 34 | Tyneham Cap | 21 | Tyneham Village | 30 |
| Studland Heath | 43 | White Nothe | 26 | Wareham | 52 |
| | | Worbarrow Bay | 29 | Worth Matravers | 35, 48 |